LECTURES ON FASCISM

AAKAR BOOKS CLASSICS

LECTURES ON FASCISM

Palmiro Togliatti

Lectures on Fascism
Palmiro Togliatti

First Aakar Edition 2021
Reprinted 2021

ISBN 978-93-5002-694-6

Published by
AAKAR BOOKS
28 E Pocket IV, Mayur Vihar Phase I
Delhi 110 091, India
www.aakarbooks.com

Printed at
Sapra Brothers, Noida

contents

foreword

THE LECTURES published here represent the bulk of a fifteen-part course on "The Adversaries" that Palmiro Togliatti gave at the Italian division of the Lenin school in Moscow in 1935. Photocopies of the original text of eight lectures were given by the Marxism-Leninism Institute of Moscow to Ernesto Ragioneri, who is currently supervising the publication of Togliatti's *Collected Works* for Editori Riuniti, and appeared in book form for the first time in Italy in 1970. Since then, the text of three more lectures—one on fascism, the remaining two on the Italian Communists' other "adversaries" (the Socialists and Republicans, and the anarchists)—have been received and published in Italy. The present volume contains only those lectures dealing with fascism and the various aspects of the fascist regime. An article on the subject which Togliatti wrote for the theoretical journal of the Communist International in 1934 is included as an appendix.

The extensive notes that constitute the text were taken by Giuseppe Gaddi, one of the students who followed the cycle of lectures. Gaddi subsequently submitted the notes on the first lecture to Togliatti for approval. The lessons aroused considerable interest in the school and were attended, according to Stefano Schiapparelli, another Italian Communist who followed them, by "teachers and students from other parties at the school." The conspicuously didactic tone of the lectures was made necessary, however, by the background of the Italian students. As Giuseppe Gaddi recalls: "Nearly all of the students were of working-class origin, coming from the fascist prisons, with little practice at studying. This was the reason for Togliatti's constant effort to be as simple and elementary as possible, and it was also the reason for the extreme attention he gave to diction, clear and at a rather slow cadence, which enormously facilitated my recording work."

Editing of the text was limited in the Italian edition to the correction of obvious typing errors, the revision of punctuation and adjustment of a few breaks in grammatical sequence. The passages in italics were underlined in the original notes. The lectures' titles are the work of Ernesto Ragionieri, editor of the Italian edition. All numbered notes are by the translator.

DANIEL DICHTER

introduction

BY PUBLISHING these lectures of Palmiro Togliatti, International Publishers is making an important contribution to the struggle against the forces of reaction and fascism. For some this may be an interesting book from the viewpoint of history. But for the people of the United States these lectures can be lessons of history we must study and apply.

In the realm of theory and of political and ideological thought nothing can substitute for the key element of experience. The greater the body of experience one can draw on, the more perceptive, penetrating and illuminating are the conclusions and the lessons. The thoughts are even clearer if one's personal involvement and experiences are interwoven into the fabric of the general experience of the masses. The body of experience of the working class and people of each nation is of significance. But by itself it is not enough from which to draw generalized theoretical, strategic or even tactical conclusions. Conclusions become accepted lessons only when they are checked and measured against the experiences from many lands.

The drawing of generalized conclusions, the further development of theory, is of necessity a collective process.

This fact stands out clearly and sharply in every one of Togliatti's "lessons." He draws on the experiences of twelve years of struggle against fascism in Italy. The "lessons" are even more vivid because he was able to draw on the experiences of his personal involvement in the struggle.

But Togliatti takes advantage of even a much broader body of experience. He was an active participant in the continuing discussions and examinations of worldwide experiences in the struggle against fascism. These discussions went on in the committees of the Communist International. The Communist

International was a center where the experiences of each country from every corner of the world became the generalized experience. By the time Togliatti delivered his lectures Hitler-fascism had been in power for some two years. So it is natural that he would especially use the experiences of the German people and the German Communists in their struggle against Hitler-fascism. The people who made up the committees of the Communist International came from working class political parties. They represented parties who based their work, their assessments, on the revolutionary science of Marxism-Leninism. So it follows that the committees of the Communist International approached all questions from the viewpoint of the working class and of Marxism-Leninism. This approach runs like a steel wire through all of Togliatti's lectures.

Because of the nature of the challenge by monopoly capital, we in the United States cannot afford the luxury of reading these lectures as intersting history but not especially of our concern. The fact is that more than any other people the lessons from the struggle against fascism must be of our concern. These lessons are of significance because more than any other people we in the United States face the danger of fascism as a continuing challenge. We face the danger now and we are going to be forced to fight against fascism as long as we are dominated by the system of monopoly capitalism. Monopoly capitalism keeps fascism as one of the options open to it when the other forms of rule become obstacles to its drive for maximum profits.

But if we learn the lessons of history as explained and pinpointed by Togliatti we can be an important factor, together with masses in struggle, in deciding that "it will not happen here."

The very first lesson that we must draw is that the inner la. of capitalism give rise to an anti-democratic tendency that feeds the movements toward fascism. In the period of capitalism's crisis and decay Togliatti speaks about "the tendency toward reactionary policies in capitalism." When in the period of its general crisis monopoly capital cannot pursue policies of maximum corporate profits, and if democratic institutions provide even the very minimum possibilities for intervention by the people against such policies, monopoly capitalism moves to hogtie or to eliminate such structures. It moves to replace democratic structures with reactionary and military regimes. Fascism is the most brutal, devastating, developed form of such big business dictatorships.

The lectures by Comrade Togliatti provide a new dimension to the developments around Watergate because what was exposed around the Nixon Administration and Watergate was a calculated, conspiratorial process in the creation of the structure which could have led to and served as a fascist structure. This process did not start with Nixon. The framework was quite well designed. The political, military and economic power was slowly being concentrated into the exclusive Executive Branch, an Executive Branch that was beyond the reach of anyone except of course the monarchs of big business. Slowly, Congress and even the President's Cabinet were bypassed. The FBI and the CIA have become a police state apparatus, operating on the basis of pages from the handbook of German and Italian fascism. The Nixon Administration prepared executive orders for use in mass roundups of all who resisted the pro-big business reactionary policies. Not even Hitler and Mussolini had available to them such massive computerized lists of names and personal histories of anyone who had ever uttered a word of protest on any question as were available to the Nixon Administration. These lists are available to the Ford Administration to this very day. Thus, the "tendency toward reaction" was laying the basis for fascism.

The lessons pointed out by Togliatti are of such vital concern to us because while the Watergate exposés and the forced Nixon resignation dealt a blow to these reactionary forces they did not put an end to the "inherent reactionary tendency" of monopoly capitalism. The "reactionary tendency" is very much alive.

Fascism always operates under false and demagogic colors. It especially tries to cover up the fact that it is "the open dictatorship of the most reactionary section of monopoly capital."

Looking back, the discussions and debates about the definition of fascism now seem abstract mainly because the basic nature of fascism is now well known. The discussions in the Communist circles were more of a debate with erroneous concepts in other left-liberal circles, most of them reflecting the influence of the demagogy and the coverup falsehoods spread by fascism.

It was necessary to expose the falsehood that fascism was "a middle class, petty bourgeois movement." It was necessary to state the fact that the petty bourgeois sector was and remains fascism's mass base, but that it is not the political essence of fascism.

The Trotskyites put forth their attempt at confusing the issues, covering up the class roots of fascism by calling fascism a "Bonapartist movement." The right-wing socialists kept seeking and projecting some positive features in fascism.

It was necessary to define fascism as the open brutal dictatorship of the most reactionary sections of the top circles of monopoly capital, because only then was it possible to pinpoint and to direct a struggle against the real enemy. Only then was it possible to mobilize the broadest movement against fascism.

During the years of Togliatti's lectures the Socialist Party in the United States, under the influence of the Trotskyites who had infiltrated and largely captured its leadership, refused to participate in any anti-fascist movement. The leadership disguised its refusal through left demagogy that the task at hand was not a broad unity against fascism but rather that the struggle was "class against class." As was to be expected the ruling class did not mind such rhetoric, especially because such left demagogy was a factor in dividing the forces that had the potential to stop the efforts of monopoly capital in establishing their open dictatorship. "Class against class" was not a policy in the interest of the working class and it was not harmful to the interests of the capitalist class. It was empty rhetoric. But it was divisive.

It was the correct Communist assessment and definition of fascism as "the open dictatorship of the most reactionary sections of monopoly capital" that provided the base for the winning anti-fascist coalition. As a result of continuous examinations, then collective discussions, a fully rounded out, a scientifically correct definition emerged. In his historic report to the Seventh World Congress of the Communist International in 1935, Georgi Dimitrov gave the following definition of fascism as "the terroristic dictatorship of the most reactionary, most chauvinistic and most imperialistic elements of finance capital."

Possibly the most important lesson of history for us in the United States is to develop an awareness of the factors that are present in our midst today that can become the base for a fascist development.

More important than the existence of some small fascist sects is the political and ideological preparation of the mass base for fascism that is going on now. From the lessons of Italy and Germany it is clear that the ideological and political atmosphere is prepared by the general ideological forces of capitalism. The "tendency toward reaction" is reflected in these ideological preparations for fascism.

"We, the middle class, are being taxed and squeezed by big government, big labor and big business." This sounds to middle class ears like a good slogan put forth by ultra-right forces such as the racist Alabama governor, George Wallace, the ultra-reactionary former California governor, Ronald Reagan and others. The words "big business" are thrown in as a sop. They are a coverup for their efforts to create an atmosphere against the working class and the trade unions. By "big government" they mean any institution over which the public has any influence. As was the case in Italy, U.S. fascism would be the open dictatorship of big business.

"Divide and rule" is a most basic element of power when a minority rules over and exploits the majority. It has been a feature of capitalist rule from its inception. Throughout history its applications and the forms have varied, depending on the specific circumstances. In the major capitalist countries the main instruments of "divide and rule" are anti-communism, great power chauvinism, white supremacy, racism and anti-Semitism. In the political and ideological sphere the instrument has been and is anti-communism. Fascism takes these ideological instruments of capitalism and develops them into its major weapons. Gernan-Hitler-fascism made anti-communism and anti-Semitism its main political and ideological weapons. Italian fascism used anti-communism and racism as its main instruments. The brutal attack on the villages and cities of Ethiopia by Italian bombers was accompanied by the most violent, despicable racist campaign.

We in the United States must see racism as the "divide and rule" ideological poison, as it is used by big business to divide and rule today. But we must also see it as a most dangerous substance that fascism feeds upon. We must draw the basic lesson that in the United States, if we are serious about blocking the path of fascism, we must fight to burn out racism.

The gangs attacking the homes where Black families live in Boston are racist thugs. But they are also the embryo of a fascist movement. In fact they have already moved from attacking the homes of Black Americans to attacking trade unions.

In this sense we must also not be misled by the fact that some elements of anti-Semitism are "out of sight." Anti-Semitism remains a live virus on the American scene. To fight the fascist danger is to fight against anti-Semitism.

With the growth of the fascist danger there will be an increase in the campaigns of anti-communism, racism, great power chauvinism and anti-Semitism.

Capitalism has always tried to cover up the fact that it exists because it exploits the working class. Fascism takes this cover a step further. Before fascism, defenders of capitalism speak about "class collaboration." When fascism is in power they speak about "eliminating the class contradiction." This is the basis of its propaganda for a corporate state. This of course is demagogy and nonsense because as long as there is capitalism there is a class contradiction and the class struggle. So in the framework of the danger of fascism the class collaborationist policies of Meany and the AFL-CIO leadership take on an additional dimension. Thus, to fight against the danger of fascism today means to struggle against the policies of class collaboration. There is a very basic lesson in Togliatti's lectures even for the class collaborationist trade union leaders. Once fascism becomes established it destroys all trade unions, including the ones with policies of class collaboration. In their place they set up their own fascist labor-front organizations.

In studying the lessons of the struggle against fascism in Germany and Italy it is necessary to see the longer range connotations of the appearance of many new "solutions" to the problems of capitalism in the United States. "Planning" has replaced "rugged individualism" as a concept. The proposals are "planning" based on class collaboration. It is "economic planning" that is in the service of monopoly capital. It is "planning" of exploitation, of greater profits. Fascism also makes a big pitch about "planning," and it is also "planning" in the best interest of big business.

In view of the negative role of social democracy in Portugal, India and many other countries, Togliatti's discussion of the policies pursued by the leadership of the Socialist Party before and during fascism takes on added importance. In Italy as well as in Germany social democracy was a factor in preparing the advent of fascism to power. It was involved in the preparations. Because of this it is unfortunate that the "transcriber" of Togliatti's notes deleted some sections in which Togliatti discussed the role of social democracy.

Fascism does not overcome the contradictions of capitalism. For periods it smothers them. But in one way or another they continue to surface, thus opening up new possibilities for struggles against fascism. The contradictions open up the possibility of struggle, but its defeat can come only as a result of organized mass struggle.

"In conclusion," Togliatti stated, "one must not believe that the masses—regimented, organized and influenced by the Fascists—one fine day will move away from fascism spontaneously, as a matter of course, and come over to us, to the proletarian revolution. We must seek these masses out and *organize* their changeover to our side."

There are a number of formulations that Togliatti set forth about the basic policies in the struggle against fascism. He places great emphasis on "the correct position of principle," a correct estimation of the relationship of forces and "correct solutions of the tactical problems." The emphasis on the "correct position of principle" as a basis for "correct solutions of tactical problems" is a warning against slipping into positions of opportunism.

Based on the accumulation of evidence from the wealth of world experience, Togliatti draws the conclusions that:

—Fascism is a danger in the capitalist countries, but it is not an inevitable stage of development;

—Fascism cannot basically resolve the problems and contradictions of capitalism. Thus, the basic class contradiction and the class struggle will continue;

—When fascism is in power, even under the most extreme conditions, it is possible to develop a mass movement and struggle to defeat fascism;

—Fascism does not collapse from its own internal contradictions, but they can be used to defeat it.

In the lectures, Togliatti reflected on the experiences and the conclusions drawn by the committees of the Communist International up to 1934. In 1935, the Communist International convened the historic Seventh World Congress. In the main report to that Congress the heroic Communist leader, Georgi Dimitrov, who as a prisoner had challenged Hitler-fascism, brought all of the experiences and conclusions up-to-date. From the Seventh Congress of the Communist International the call went out—"Unity Against Fascism."

The lectures of Togliatti were an important feature of the collective preparations for the Seventh World Congress. Because of its work the Communist movement the world over was able to fulfill its vanguard role in the struggle against fascism. It was the Communist Parties and their policies of anti-fascist unity that created the mass base for the anti-fascism that defeated the fascist challenge.

It was not an accident of history that the lectures were delivered in the Soviet Union. The Soviet Union, a revolutionary working class socialist state, was the central force blocking the path of fascism. It was not an accident of history that the Soviet Union was the main force in militarily defeating the forces of fascism in the Second World War. It is not an accident of history that the Soviet Union and the other socialist states are today the main obstacle to the path of world imperialism and the main bastion in the struggle against fascism.

The lectures in this book are not only lessons of history. They are lessons in the use of Marxism-Leninism. They are lessons in the working class approach to all questions.

August 22, 1975 GUS HALL

General Secretary, Communist Party U.S.A.

lecture 1

The Basic Features of the Fascist Dictatorship

BEFORE beginning our course, I want to say a few words on the term "adversaries" to keep some of you from making a false interpretation of this term, a false interpretation that could lead to political errors.

When we speak of "adversaries" we do not have in mind *the masses* enrolled in the fascist, social-democratic and Catholic organizations. Our adversaries are the fascist, social-democratic and Catholic *organizations*. But the masses belonging to them are not our adversaries; they are masses of workers whom we must make every effort to win over.

Let's get on with our subject: fascism. What is fascism? What is the most complete definition that has been given of it?

The most complete definition of fascism was given by the 13th meeting of the Enlarged Executive of the Communist International and is as follows: "Fascism is the open terrorist dictatorship of the most reactionary, most chauvinistic, most imperialist elements of finance capital."

Fascism has not always been defined this way. Diverse, often erroneous definitions have been given of fascism at diverse stages and at different times. It would be interesting (and it's a job I advise you to undertake) to study the diverse definitions we have given of fascism at various stages.

At the Fourth World Congress, for example, Clara Zetkin delivered a speech on fascism that was almost entirely dedicated to pointing out its petty-bourgeois character. Bordiga,[1] instead, insisted on seeing no difference whatever between bourgeois democracy and fascist dictatorship, making them appear almost like the same thing, saying that between these two forms of bourgeois government there is a kind of rotation, of alternation.

These speeches lacked an effort to unite, to connect two elements: the dictatorship of the bourgeoisie and the movement of the petty-bourgeois masses.

From the theoretical point of view, what is hard is to fully grasp the link between these two elements. Yet this link must be understood. If one stops at the first element, one does not see, one loses sight of the main line of fascism's historical development and its class content; if one stops at the second element, one loses sight of the prospects.

This is an error social democracy committed. Until a short time ago, social democracy denied everything we said about fascism, regarding it as a return to medieval forms, as a degeneration of bourgeois society. Social democracy based these definitions exclusively on the petty-bourgeois mass character that fascism had actually assumed.

But the movement of the masses isn't the same in every country. Not even the dictatorship is the same in every country. This is why I must forewarn you of an error that is easily made. Do not think that what is true for Italy must also be true, must hold, for every other country. Fascism can take different forms in different countries. The masses of different countries have different forms of organization too. And we must also bear in mind the period of which we are speaking. Fascism assumes different aspects at different times in the same country. Hence, we must consider two elements. We have already seen the most complete definition of fascism: "Fascism is the open terrorist dictatorship of the most reactionary, most chauvinistic, most imperialist elements of finance capital."

What does this mean? And why, at this precise moment, at this stage of historical development, are we confronted with this form, that is to say with the open, undisguised dictatorship of the most reactionary and most chauvinistic strata of the bourgeoisie?

It is necessary to speak of this because not everyone is clear on this problem. I encountered a comrade whose head was so filled with this definition that he was astonished to learn that one of Gramsci's articles said that every state is a dictatorship.

Clearly, bourgeois democracy and dictatorship cannot be set in contraposition. Every democracy is a dictatorship.

Let us see what position the German Social Democrats took in defining fascism. They said fascism wrests power from the big bourgeoisie and passes it to the petty bourgeoisie, which then uses it against the former. You can also find this position in all the Italian Social Democratic writers: Turati, Treves, etc.[2] From this position they derived their strategy, according to which the struggle against fascism will be waged by all the social strata, etc. This is how they evaded the problem of the proletariat's function in the struggle against fascism.

But let's come up in time. In 1932 in Germany, a number of opposition currents, including fringe groups in the Communist Party, asserted that fascism installs the dictatorship of the petty bougeoisie on the big bourgeoisie. This was an incorrect assumption from which an incorrect political orientation inevitably was derived. It can be found in all the writings of the "Right-wingers." In this connection, I also want to put you on guard against another definition. Watch out when you hear fascism spoken of as "Bonapartism." This proposition, which is Trotskyism's warhorse, is drawn from some statements by Marx (in *The 18th Brumaire*, etc.) and Engels; but Marx and Engels' analyses, valid at the time for that era of capitalism's development, become incorrect when mechanically applied today, in the age of imperialism.

What follows from this definition of fascism as "Bonapartism"? What stems from it is the conclusion that it isn't the bourgeoisie that is in command, but Mussolini and the generals, who wrested power from the bourgeoisie too.

Remember the way Trotsky defined the Brüning government: "a Bonapartist government."[3] The Trotskyites have always had this conception of fascism. What is its root? Its root is the disavowal of the definition of fascism as the dictatorship of the bourgeoisie.

Why has fascism, the open dictatorship of the bourgeoisie,

arisen today, precisely in this period? You can find the answer in Lenin himself; you should look for it in his works on imperialism. *You can't know what fascism is if you don't know imperialism.*

You know the economic features of imperialism. You know the definition Lenin gives. Imperialism is characterized by: 1) the concentration of production and capital, the formation of monopolies which play a decisive role in economic life; 2) the merging of bank capital with industrial capital, and the creation, on the basis of finance capital, of a financial oligarchy; 3) the great importance acquired by the export of capital; 4) the rise of international capitalist monopolies, and, lastly, the repartitioning of the world among the great capitalist powers, which can now be viewed as complete.

These are the features of imperialism. Based on them, there is a tendency of all the bourgeoisie's political institutions to undergo a reactionary transformation. This, too, you will find in Lenin. There is a tendency to make these institutions reactionary, and this tendency appears in its most coherent forms with fascism.

Why? Because, given the class relations and the capitalists' need to safeguard their profits, the bourgeoisie must find forms with which to exert heavy pressure on the workers. Furthermore, the monopolies, that is to say the bourgeosie's leading forces, reach their highest degree of concentration, and the old forms of rule become impediments to their expansion. The bourgeoisie must turn against what it itself created, because what once was a factor of its development today has become an obstacle to the preservation of capitalist society.

This is why the bourgeoisie must turn reactionary and resort to fascism.

At this point I must caution you against another error: schematism. You must be careful not to consider the transition from bourgeois democracy to fascism fatal and inevitable. Why? Because imperialism does not *necessarily* have to give birth to the fascist dictatorship. Let's look at some practical examples. England, for instance, is a great imperialist state in which there is a democratic parliamentary regime (although here, too, it cannot be said that reactionary features are not present). Take France, the United States, etc. In these countries you will find tendencies toward the fascist form of society, but the parlimentary forms still exist. This tendency toward the fascist form of government is present everywhere, but this still does not mean fascism must perforce be arrived at everywhere.

If we were to argue a similar proposition, we would be making a schematic error, affirming as true that which does not exist in reality; and at the same time we would be making a gross political error inasmuch as we would fail to see that the probabilities of establishing a fascist dictatorship depend on the degree of the fighting spirit of the working class and its ability to defend the democratic institutions. When the proletariat is opposed, it's hard to overthrow these institutions. This struggle to defend the democratic institutions broadens and becomes the struggle for power.

This is the first element to spell out in defining fascism.

The second element consists in the nature of fascism's mass organizations. The term fascism is often used imprecisely as a synonym for reaction, terror, etc. This is incorrect. Fascism does not denote only the struggle against bourgeois democracy; we cannot use this expression when we are confronted with that struggle alone. We must use it only when the fight against the working class develops on a new mass base with a petty-bourgeois character, as we can see in Germany, Italy, France, England—anywhere a typical fascism exists.

Hence, the fascist dictatorship endeavors to possess a mass movement by organizing the bourgeoisie and petty bourgeoisie.

It is very difficult to connect these two movements. It is very difficult not to stress one to the detriment of the other. For example, when Italian fascism was developing, before the March on Rome, the Party ignored this important problem: to keep the big bourgeoisie from winning over the discontented petty-bourgeois masses. At the time, these masses were made up of ex-servicemen, of several strata of poor peasants on the way to becoming wealthy, and of a whole mass of misfits created by the war.

We didn't understand that there was an Italian social phenomenon underlying all this; we didn't see the deep-going social causes determining it; we didn't understand that the ex-servicemen, the misfits, were not isolated individuals but a *mass,* and represented a phenomenon having class aspects; we didn't understand that we could not simply tell them to go to the devil! Thus, for example, having returned home, the misfits, who had exercised command during the war, wanted to continue to give orders, criticized the existing order and raised a whole series of problems that we should have taken into consideration.

Our job was to win over a part of this mass and neutralize the other, thereby preventing it from becoming a mass maneuvered by the bourgeoisie. We neglected these tasks.

This was one of our errors, an error that has been repeated elsewhere as well: to overlook the shift of the intermediate strata and the creation of trends in the petty bourgeoisie that the bourgeoisie can use against the working class.

Another error of ours was not to always stress sufficiently the fascist dictatorship's class character. We pointed to capitalism's weakness as the reason for the fascist dictatorship. A speech by Bordiga strongly emphasized the role of the weakest elements of capitalism—the rural bourgeoisie—in creating fascism. From this premise we deduced that fascism is a regime characteristic of countries with a weak capitalist economy. This error is explained in part by the fact that we were the first to have to cope with fascism. Later, we saw how fascism developed in Germany, etc.

But at the same time we committed another error. In defining the nature of the Italian economy, we limited ourselves to seeing how much was produced in the countryside and how much was produced in the cities.

We did not allow for the fact that Italy is one of the countries where industry and finance are most highly concentrated; we did not allow for the fact that it wasn't enough to consider agriculture's role, but that, instead, we should have seen the very advanced organic composition of Italian capital. It should have been sufficient to see the concentration, the monopolies, etc., in order to draw the conclusion that Italian capitalism was not a weak capitalism after all.

We were not the only ones to commit this error. This error might be termed general.

For example, a similar error was made in Germany in judging the fascist movement's development in 1931. Some comrades asserted that fascism had been beaten back; that there was no threat of fascist dictatorship because such a danger did not exist in a country as developed as Germany, where the working-class forces were so well developed. We have barred the road to fascism, they said. Allusions to this also can be found in several speeches at the 11th meeting of the Enlarged Executive. This is the same error we made: to underestimate the fascist mass movement's growth potential. In 1932 the same comrades felt that the fascist dictatorship had already been established under the Brüning government, and that, therefore, there was no further need to fight the fascist movement.

This, too, was an error. They viewed fascism only as the reactionary transformation of the bourgeois institutions. But the Brüning government was not yet a fascist dictatorship. It lacked one of the ingredients: a reactionary mass base enabling it to successfully fight to the finish against the working class and thus clear the ground for the open fascist dictatorship.

You see, when the analysis is wrong, the political orientation will be wrong too.

Another problem arises in this regard: does the establishment of a fascist dictatorship represent a strengthening or weakening of the bourgeoisie?

This was much discussed, especially in Germany. Some comrades mistakenly contended that the fascist dictatorship is only a sign of the weakening of the bourgeoisie. They said: the bourgeoisie resorts to fascism because it cannot govern with the old systems, and this is a sign of weakness.

It's true, fascism does develop because the internal contradictions have reached such a point that the bourgeoisie is compelled to liquidate the democratic forms. From this point of view, it means that we are confronted with a profound crisis, that a revolutionary crisis is brewing which the bourgeoisie wants to meet. But to see only this side leads us to mistakenly draw this conclusion: that the more the fascist movement grows, the more acute the revolutionary crisis becomes.

The comrades who reasoned this way did not see the second element, the mobilization of the petty bourgeoisie. And they did not see that this mobilization, this element, contained factors strengthening the bourgeoisie inasmuch as it permitted it to govern with methods different from the democratic ones.

Another mistake was to lapse into fatalism. This concept was expressed by Radek, who said these comrades think Marx's affirmation that between capitalism and socialism there is a period of transition, represented by the dictatorship of the proletariat, should be superseded by the affirmation that between capitalism and socialism there must be a period of fascist dictatorship.

This mistake results in the loss of perspective and the belief that everything is over once fascism has seized power. Look, instead, at what has happened in France. The gathering of the bourgeoisie's forces has been answered by the concentration of the proletariat's forces. The Communist Pary has expertly raised a roadblock to the advent of fascism. Today, in France, the problem of fascism no longer is the same as it was on February 6;[4] the balance of forces has changed. The threat of fascism hasn't passed, but it has been fought, which in itself has aggravated the bourgeoisie's crisis. Fascism is getting ready to counterattack, to launch a new offensive; we must organize our forces to repel it. And we cannot comprehend the problem if we do not see it this way: as class struggle; as the struggle between the bourgeoisie and the proletariat in which the bourgeoisie has at stake the establishment of its dictatorship, in its most open form, and the proletariat has at stake the establishment of its own dictatorship, which it arrives at by fighting in the defense of all its democratic rights.

This is why Bordiga was wrong when he scornfully asked: why should we fight for democratic rights? After all, these things can go to the devil in the current period. . . . Lenin, in polemics with Bukharin and Pyatakov over the Party program, had already provided an answer to his question in 1919. Bukharin and Pyatakov maintained that, since the phase of imperialism had been reached, it was no longer necessary for the program to take the earlier stages into account. But Lenin replied: no, we have passed these stages, but that does not mean the gains the working class made during them are without value. The proletariat must fight to defend these gains. The battle front for the proletariat's victory is welded in this struggle.

Let's look now at another question, the question of fascist ideology. What does it represent in this struggle?

When we analyze this ideology, what do we find? Everything. It is an eclectic ideology. An element common to all fascist movements everywhere is a vehement nationalist ideology. It's not necessary to speak at length with regard to Italy. This element is even stronger in Germany because Germany is a nation which was defeated in the war, and the nationalist element lent itself even more readily to rallying the masses.

Besides this element there are numerous fragments derived from other sources; for example, from social democracy. The corporative ideology, for instance, whose underlying principle is class collaboration, isn't an invention of fascism but of social democracy. But there are still other elements which do not come from social democracy either; for example, the conception of capitalism (not common to all fascisms, but one you will find in the Italian, German and French versions) according to which imperialism is a degeneration that must be eliminated, while the true capitalist economy is that of the original period, and so there must be a return to the origins. You will find this conception in a number of democratic currents, for instance in *Giustizia e Libertà*.[5] This is not a social-democratic, but a *romantic* ideology revealing the petty bourgeoisie's effort to make the world, which is moving forward toward socialism, turn back.

New concepts are arising in fascist ideology in Italy and Germany. In Italy, there is talk of going beyond capitalism by giving it elements of organization. Here, the social-democratic element turns up again, but they also rob from Communism (planning, etc.).

Fascist ideology contains a series of heterogeneous ingredients. We must bear this in mind because this trait enables us to understand the purpose this ideology serves. It serves to solder together various factions in the struggle for dictatorship over the working masses and to create a vast movement for this scope. *Fascist ideology is an instrument created to bind these elements together.*

A part of the ideology—the nationalist part—directly serves the bourgeoisie; the other acts as a bond.

I warn you against the tendency to regard fascist ideology as something that is solidly formed, complete, homogeneous. Nothing more closely resembles a chameleon than fascist ideology. *Don't look at fascist ideology without considering the objectives which fascism proposes to reach at a given moment with a given ideology.*

Its fundamental line remains vehement nationalism and the analogy with social democracy. Why this analogy? Because social-democratic ideology is also a petty-bourgeois ideology, that is to say the petty-bourgeois content is common to both ideologies; but this analogy expresses itself in different forms at different times in different countries.

Let's rapidly lay the groundwork for the next lesson. How, in Italy, at a specific moment, was the problem of organizing the fascist dictatorship posed, and how was the reactionary movement organized? This is the subject.

Let's go back to the origins. On the one hand there is the revolutionary crisis. The bourgeoisie is unable to rule with the old systems. There is general discontent, a working-class offensive, political strikes, general strikes, etc. In short, we are in the postwar period—the deep revolutionary crisis.

One factor especially stands out: the impossibility for the Italian ruling class to apply the old policy, the policy applied up to 1912, Giolitti's "reformist" policy;[6] not reformist because the reformists were in power, but because it was a policy of concessions to certain groups, aimed at keeping the bourgeois dictatorship alive in its parliamentary guise.

This policy no longer stands up in the postwar period because the masses of workers and peasants rebel against it.

Two major developments can be noted in the postwar period: the great growth of the Italian Socialist Party, which counts hundreds of thousands of members and millions of voters; and the reawakening of the peasant classes, divided among many parties because the peasants are fragmented. The Popular Party[7] is a peasant party. At the same time we see peasant movements, land takeovers in the South, etc.

The workers and peasants move to the attack and their bloc begins to form. This confluence of the working-class and peasant attacks can be found in its most advanced forms in postwar Italy. It signals the end of the parliamentary forms.

The bourgeoisie must liquidate parliamentarianism. Discontent is spread not only to the workers, but also encompasses the petty bourgeoisie. Petty-bourgeois, ex-servicemen's and other movements spring up. The bourgeoisie and petty bourgeoisie no longer can tolerate the existing regime; they want to change it.

This is the ground on which fascism arises.

When is this movement among the petty bourgeoisie transformed into a unified movement? Not at the beginning, but at the end of 1920. It is transformed when a new factor intervenes; when the most reactionary forces of the bourgeoisie intervene as an organizing factor. Fascism had been growing before, but had not yet become the fundamental element.

The fascist movement arises during the war. Later, it continues in the *fasci di combattimento.*[8] Some individuals, however, would not follow it to the very end. For example, in polemics with Nenni, we call him a Fascist, but at a certain point he left the movement.[9] At the outset, fascism was made up of various unhomogeneous groups which would not march together to the finish. Observe the fascist movement's chapters in the cities. In 1919-20 you will find petty-bourgeois elements, members of various parties, discussing general political problems, raising a series of questions, putting forth demands. This is the context in which fascism's first program is born. The Piazza San Sepolcro program[10] is predominantly petty-bourgeois, reflecting the orientation of the urban *fasci.* Take fascism in the countryside, in Emilia, etc., instead. It is different; it appears later on, in 1920, taking the form of squads armed for the fight against the working class. *It arises as* squadrismo.[11] Misfits, petty bourgeois, intermediate social strata adhere to it. But it is immediately an organ of struggle against the working class: no discussions are carried on in its headquarters. Why this difference? Because *here the rural bourgeoisie intervened at once as an organizing factor.*

Starting in mid-1921 squads are also formed in the cities; first in Trieste, where the nationalist problem is sharpest, then in the other cities where the forces are most tense. The squads are forged on the rural model. They are formed in Turin after the occupation of the factories,[12] while in Emilia, instead, fascism already has a strong organization by this time.

Toward the end of 1920 the bourgeoisie also intervenes in the cities as an organizing factor and the fascist squads appear. A series of crises opens within the fascist movement, the crisis of the first two years.

It is debated: *are we a party*? This is the problem of the Rome Congress, the Congress at the Augusteo.[13] The Congress says: we must become a party. Mussolini answers: let's still remain a movement. Mussolini tried to hold together the broadest possible masses, which is why he always enjoyed greater favor. The fight was between those who openly wanted to demolish the organizations of the working class and those in whom there still were large vestiges of the old ideologies.

Mussolini betrays the D'Annunzio movement, which could have been dangerous.[14] In 1920 he takes a sympathetic attitude to the occupation of the factories, but then changes completely. The first open contacts are made between the fascist movement and the industrialists' organizations. The offensive begins. It will last two years, until the March on Rome.

The factor of organization had intervened. The rural bourgeoisie had supplied the squadrista *form of organization and the industrialists had then applied it in the cities.*

The correctness of what we have maintained concerning the two elements—the petty-bourgiois forces and the organizational factor constituted by the big bourgeoisie—can be deduced from this analysis.

We will see how these elements have influenced each other.

lecture 2

The Bourgeoisie's "New Type of Party"

IN THE first part of our lesson, as you will recall, we attempted to correctly define fascism, basing ourselves on documents of the International and on the Italian experience. We attempted to throw an exact light on the fundamental elements of the fascist dictatorship, emphasizing its class character—the fact that it is the expression of the most reactionary sectors of the bourgeoisie—and insisting on the second element, which consists in the petty-bourgeois mass movement this dictatorship has been able to attract.

The whole lesson was dedicated to combating errors which are made with reference to fascism; errors by which fascism is not viewed in its development since its various elements and their interrelationships are not seen.

Part of the lesson was devoted to the function of fascist ideology, which we depicted as a confused, eclectic ideology which serves to hold together the petty-bourgeois strata belonging to the fascist movement.

We warned against errors of schematism. Today, I want to begin by again warning you against errors of schematism in connection with one of the problems of the history of fascism in Italy.

It is a grave error to believe that fascism started out in 1920, or from the March on Rome, with a pre-established, predetermined plan for the dictatorial regime, as this regime has been organized in the course of ten years, and as we see it today. This would be a grave error.

All the historical facts of fascism's development contradict such a conception. What's more, if one embraces this conception, one inevitably falls into fascist ideology; it means that in one way or another one is already under the direct or indirect influence of fascism. It is the Fascists, in fact, who try to show that everything they have done has been based on pre-established plans.

As we have said, this is not true. However, it is important to dwell on this so as to learn to combat this error, since in combating it we are combating possible deviations in the political sphere.

We must oppose the true, the correct conception of the fascist dictatorship to this mistaken conception. The fascist dictatorship has been driven to assume its current forms by objective factors, by real factors—by the economic situation and the mass movements this situation has brought into being. With this, we don't mean to say that the factor of organization does not intervene; but woe if we confine ourselves to seeing this factor and do not refer to the objective situation, to the real situation created at any given moment. The bourgeoisie has always intervened as a factor of organization.

If we do not do so, we cannot determine what the political possibilities are with any exactness and set the line of action we want to pursue, the line which must govern the Party's action. You can understand the importance of this: if, at a given time, a mass movement had been able to intervene one way rather than another, the dictatorship would have assumed different forms.

If, during the Matteotti crisis,[1] the masses had intervened differently than they actually did, the situation no doubt would have taken a different turn. We can also see this today. When our Party intervenes more actively, it forces fascism to grapple with certain problems: modification of the trade-union structure, amnesty, the problem of the youth *fasci*, reorganization of the National Fascist Party, attempts to compromise with social democracy, etc.

Fascism has taken all of its positions on these problems in its reaction to mass movements. If one does not see this, one inevitably falls—if one hasn't already fallen—under the influence of fascism and into revolutionary pessimism. Such revolutionary pessimism is very widespread in Italy among the petty-bourgeois strata, which accept and recognize as fact the notion that fascism had to take this path perforce, that fascism could not have taken any other path, that the one it has taken was inevitable.

We must combat this point of view, for only by combating it can we see how fascism's prospects of development are tied to the prospects of the economic situation and of the class struggle.

Fascism's prospects of development are not set today; they are not advancing along a pre-established course. Today, as always, these prospects are tied to the prospects of the economic situation and of the class struggle.

Let's document this. We shall insist on this throughout the entire course, since it would be the end if we regarded fascism's current prospects as fixed, established, lasting, permanent. We must always bear in mind that the state machine is nothing but a political superstructure derived from class relations.

Let's take the development of fascism in Italy to illustrate this point.

I would divide this study into three periods: first, fascism up to the March on Rome, up to the end of 1922; second, from 1922 to 1925, which can be defined as the period of the attempt to create a non-totalitarian fascist regime; third, from 1925 to 1930, the period of the foundation of totalitarianism and of the opening of the great economic crisis.

The most evident feature of the period going up to the March on Rome was fascism's lack of any definite program. If you look at fascism's successive positions from 1919 to 1922, you will see they varied continually. You are aware of what the situation was in this period; we have already spoken of it. Let's underscore again several elements: deep-going revolutionary crisis; breakdown of the basic political institutions; general discontent, particularly among the great masses of workers and peasants; and the tendency of the revolutionary working-class and peasant forces, pushing for a change in the situation, to join together forming a bloc.

What was the bourgeoisie's program for saving itself in this period? The bourgeoisie adopted different programs at different moments.

The first program was that of Nitti,[2] a representative of finance capital in its most typical form. Nitti was the man of the big banks, the one who organized the largest Italian bank, the Discount Bank. But Nitti was also the man of the most progressive, forward-looking democracy. In Nitti's program we find the union of two elements—the supremacy of finance capital and a democratic program; two elements which at first glance seem contradictory, the former favoring finance capitalism and the latter being a very advanced element of social demagogy.

What did this program represent? It represented the bourgeoisie's attempt to find a way out of the situation. Nitti foresaw a profound transformation of society. He did not exclude a transition to republican forms of government, nor did he exclude a constituent assembly. He did not exclude collaborating not only with the Popular Party, but with the Socialists as well.

Nitti continued the policy of granting concessions to certain groups with the intent of corrupting them, but he tried to broaden this policy, to grant concessions to more progressive forces.

He had created the Royal Guard, yielding in this to the wishes of the most reactionary elements of the bourgeoisie, and he later used it to buttress his position; but, at the same time, he fornicated with social democracy, discussed progressive economic measures, etc.

Compare his program with the original program of the *fasci di combattimento*, the Piazza San Sepolcro program of 1919. They tally on nearly every point. The program of the *fasci* was a republican program, while Nitti's contained much talk of a Republic; the program of the *fasci* spoke of a constituent assembly, and Nitti did not count this out; the former spoke of anti-capitalist measures such as a graduated tax on capital, etc., measures which Nitti, too, had mentioned.

In this you can see the Italian bourgeoisie's attempt in 1919 and in the early months of 1920 to overcome the crisis through very advanced political maneuvers, an attempt reflected in the 1919 program of the *fasci di combattimento*.

Nitti's plan failed, however; it was not realized. The situation was such as to render its implementation impossible. It collided with a series of contradictory factors and inevitably ground to a halt in the face of insurmountable political obstacles.

At bottom, the ones who really wrecked Nitti's program were the proletariat and Southern peasants. These masses, which were the target of the bourgeoisie's advanced reformist maneuvers, were raising even more advanced problems: the problem of power, the problem of seizing land, etc. The farm workers of Emilia, a region where the labor unions were then at the height of their expansion, were raising problems which shook the very foundations of private property in the countryside, which shook all the bases on which society rests. Nitti's program was a utopian program that inescapably was forced to founder.

So the bourgeoisie then made another attempt. The bourgeoisie's second attempt in the postwar period was to try to get out of the situation with Giolitti.[3] Giolitti was an old bourgeois statesman. During the war he had been a defeatist traitor (!). He, too, had taken quasi-republican positions, as, for example, in his Dronero speech, in which he proposed changing the Constitution in order to divest the king of the power to declare war. Yet he had been the monarchy's most loyal man. It can be said that it was he who had organized the monarchy along modern lines. Still and all, he, too, tended to take republican positions.

But Giolitti's program differed from Nitti's in a certain respect. Giolitti came to power when Nitti's program had already failed.

You can find two ingredients in Giolitti's program: on the one hand, the importance of fascism and the importance of seizing on it as an armed movement to crush the proletariat; on the other, the plan to crush the Socialist Party—to drive out the revolutionaries, isolate the reformists and co-opt them into the government.

Giolitti's program, as he tried to apply it in 1921 and up to the start of 1922, was a political program of parliamentary collaboration between the old forces of the reactionary ruling classes and the two big parties that had arisen in the postwar period, the

Socialist and Popular parties. But, as we have seen, Giolitti's program also leaned on the fascist movement for support, regarding it as an armed movement for smashing the proletarian strongholds.

It can be said that Giolitti's formula was the one propounded by *La Stampa*[4] of Turin: what's needed is a Giolitti-Mussolini-Turati government.

What was happening at this time? The decisive strata of the Italian bourgeoisie were becoming aware of the impossibility of getting out of the situation without an armed struggle. After the occupation of the factories, they adhered to fascism. This, then, was the political and social basis of Giolitti's program—an attempt to overcome the situation with forms of this kind.

What was the Fascist Party doing in this period? Pay close attention. Within the Fascist Party you will see the same shifts that occurred within the bourgeoisie. The 1919 program of the *fasci di combattimento* began to be set aside, fascism entered Parliament as a political party, and Mussolini intervened in Parliament with a speech that was not the least bit revolutionary: he anticipated a government of collaboration with the Socialists.

Fascism orients itself in accordance with the line laid down by the decisive strata of the bourgeoisie. You can see here that the decisions are always made by these decisive strata of the bourgeoisie. The form may change, but the substance always remains the same.

This situation found political expression in the pacification pact.[5] Mussolini fought in the Fascist Party for the pacification pact with the Socialists. The Socialists—the Communists having left the party[6]—accepted the pact under pressure from the right wing. Mussolini signed it, and on it you will also find the signatures of the socialist movement's most prominent leaders..

Nevertheless, these plans—Giolitti's program—failed as well. Why? Because the same factor that had wrecked Nitti's social plan intervened: the masses intervened. The masses' response to Giolitti's plan was to unleash their counteroffensive, their resistance to fascism's offensive: we have the *Arditi del popolo*.[7] The *Arditi del popolo* were of fundamental political importance.

They represented one of the elements that destroyed Giolitti's plan.

The pacification pact was short-lived. The rural bourgeoisie, heavy industry and finance worked to destroy it. The Nationalists, more intransigent than Mussolini, called for a fight to the finish to demolish the proletarian organizations.

The plan, therefore, came to nothing. The right-wingers of the Socialist Party couldn't join the government since the direct consequence of this would have been their isolation. They would have found themselves cut off from millions of workers belonging to the General Confederation of Labor. The workers would have abandoned them, and in the government they would have represented no one but themselves. When Turati finally went to the Quirinal Palace,[8] he was a mere shadow. He no longer represented anything; he represented not a force, but impotence.

This plan having failed, only one path remained: the March on Rome. With this, we can see how the statements of those who say the March on Rome was also carried out against a part of the bourgeoisie, that the generals were ready to open fire, etc., are nonsense. They do not fit the facts.

It's true that there had been a big struggle within the bourgeoisie, that many had opposed Giolitti's return to power; but this struggle among the various strata of the bourgeoisie only reflected the struggle of the masses.

The decisive strata of the bourgeoisie—the banks, big industry, the General Staff—all were in league with fascism in the March on Rome. Even the monarchy was on similar ground, for the court had already raised and settled the problem of fascism. What's more, the Vatican also was backing fascism. The decisive strata therefore were in agreement; their line was fascism.

A series of rather important changes occurred at this time within the Fascist Party, the chief one doubtless being the liquidation of the republican question. This prejudicial question was liquidated in the Udine speech[9] only three weeks before the March on Rome. The Fascist Party thereby presented itself as a government party in that moment in the Italian situation.

Meanwhile, the offensive had been unleashed against the critical points of proletarian resistance and had broken them. The proletarian strongholds of Emilia and Tuscany were burned to the ground; the Socialist-run towns and cities, in their overwhelming majority, were stormed; the revolutionary movement of the national minorities was completely wiped out in the Trent region, while the most unbridled terror was loosed in Trieste. Thus, the positions crucial to the strength of the Italian proletarian movement were obliterated. There was no other way out for the bourgeoisie; no longer could any other organized bourgeois force propose a different plan.

What other plan might there have been? There was but one: the revolutionary struggle of the proletariat. This was the only solution. We had opened up possibilities far exceeding those which we exploited. Just think of the *Arditi del popolo*, for example. But by then, at the time of the March on Rome, the balance of forces had already tipped plainly against us.

A better, more correct Communist Party policy line could have given us greater possibilities, could have sharpened the fight. A Communist Party policy capable of uniting all the discontented masses and assembling them in a broad battle front no doubt would have changed the situation and reopened possibilities of revolutionary crisis.

But in that given moment the balance of forces was against us.

Why have I mentioned this problem? I have done so in order to refer back to what I said at the beginning and to illustrate it: the duel with fascism never must be thought of as over and done. Look at France on February 6.[10] Some might have said the game was up; the situation took the Party by surprise. But the Party recovered at once and, with a skillful united-front policy, knew how to put itself at the head of the popular masses, give them drive, lead them into the fight against fascism, build a barrier against fascism's offensive.

We must never forget this. Every time the Communist Party is able to find a crack, a fissure in fascism, it must drive a wedge into it, in order to render the situation mobile again and thus reopen the possibilities of struggle.

What was fascism's program after the March on Rome? A new period opened in the Fascist Party at this time—the period of the attempt to build a non-totalitarian fascist regime.

When Mussolini was appointed to form the government after the March on Rome, he didn't think even for an instant of forming an all-Fascist cabinet. He formed a cabinet of parliamentary collaboration and even offered the Socialists a place in it.

I remember speaking with Buozzi and Baldesi[11] in Parliament one day. "Mussolini," they told me, "has offered us a place in the government. What can we do? We are under the enemy's gun; we must accept." If they did not enter the government, no praise is due them. It was the bourgeoisie that didn't want it. Time had run out on the Giolittian plan of collaboration.

The middle-level Fascist Party cadres—the *squadristi*—on the one hand, and the Nationalists, representing the most reactionary elements of the bourgeoisie, on the other, intervened against the attempt to bring the Socialists into the government.

Still, the attempt was made. And—note well—it foundered and failed in the face of a series of objective difficulties and real problems, the solution to which compelled fascism to forge ahead in organizing the dictatorship.

We are now in 1922, '23 '24, approaching the period of relative stabilization. All the problems of the relative stabilization were posed in Italy. What could fascism do? It could only carry out the orders of its master, the bourgeoisie. The first crisis opened, one which we can say was always present in this period: a crisis set off by conflicts between fascism's policy and its original mass base. The cadres and rank and file either remained attached to the old program or had ideas about the takeover of power which were not shared by the bourgeoisie.

Take the *Arditi*, the squad captains, the misfits, the officers. As a social group, they had been waiting to take power for some time. Power, once seized, was to have been theirs. These groups fed on the utopian conception that the petty bourgeoisie can take power and lay down the law to the proletariat and the bourgeoisie, organize society according to its own plans, etc.

When fascism came to power, this conception had to be smacked down by reality. Once in power, fascism's first acts were econonic measures favoring the bourgeoisie. Here we must not oversimplify. There was no immediate attack on wages. Not even in Germany has a large-scale attack on wages been loosed so far. Why? Because the bourgeoisie cannot tackle all the problems simultaneously. At the time, the bourgeoisie faced the problem of reorganizing the state apparatus; of curbing the discontent of the petty bourgeoisie, which was constantly making new demands and was surging into the state apparatus; and of still dealing with the working masses, which had been beaten, but which could easily regroup their forces under the pressure of the bourgeoisie's offensive.

At first, the bourgeoisie tried to hold back the class struggle, to keep this element from intervening and becoming a predominant element. The bourgeoisie was helped by the stabilization inasmuch as it was given a chance to solve certain economic problems. The war apparatus tying industry's hands was dismantled; all the restrictive measures taken in the preceding period were lifted, giving capital the broadest freedom, bolstering its initiative, etc.

The objective factor that permitted fascism to handle the various problems without sharpening the class issue with an offensive against wages consisted precisely in the fact that its seizure of power coincided with the beginning of the stabilization, with a period of improvement in the Italian economic situation, with an upswing.

Nonetheless, this still was the most trying period for fascism—the most trying because it was in this period that the contradictions between fascism's program and the aspirations of the petty-bourgeois masses tied to its original program surfaced. How did these difficulties, these contradictions, reveal themselves in the first year?

They were revealed in the simmering of opposition movements outside the fascist camp. These movements tended to attract the forces of the petty bourgeoisie, even those inside the fascist camp, which was thus forced to lead a fight against them. If it had tolerated them, fascism would have seen its mass base profoundly shaken.

Fascism squared off first against the Popular Party; the Popular Party was the first enemy against which it had to aim its blows. Cabinet ministers belonging to the Popular Party were openly taking opposition stands. Next, it had to turn on other groups and parties that had formed and were taking a position hostile to fascism. These groups and parties had a strong base in the petty- and middle-bourgeois strata particularly hard hit by the measures fascism had taken—measures which were beginning the economic concentration, ruining small property owners, increasing the weight of taxation on small peasants, etc. Discontent became especially grave during this period, reached up to the very confines of, and even penetrated within, the Fascist Party. It was the sum of two elements: dissatisfaction, and the difficulty in gaining mastery over the state apparatus right from the outset and making it run properly by replacing the old men. The Matteotti crisis sprang from these difficulties.

At the start of the Matteotti crisis, the working class did not appear as the dominant factor. This is demonstrated by a series of facts; for example, there was greater ferment in the South, in Rome, in Naples, than in Turin. Only later did the working class intervene, regathering its forces and becoming the dominant factor. Only in 1925-26 did our Party move to the fore and truly become a vanguard.

Why? Because the objective situation, the character of the stabilization of Italian capitalism, fully revealed itself. The offensive against the workers and the attack on wages began, unemployment grew, the cost of living rose, and, especially the process of the concentration and centralization of the economy and of production assumed greater intensity at this particular time. Buoyed by this growing concentration of the economy, the bourgeois ruling classes began the most advanced process of unification, based on unity in the sharper offensive against the organization of the working class.

I said the origins of the Matteotti crisis must be sought in the conflict between the wavering elements of the big bourgeoisie at the center and of the petty bourgeoisie at the base. The proletariat stepped in as a decisive factor only at the last moment. A series of objective factors—economic and class factors—also intervened at the same time. For example, the stabilization—capital's freedom to expand—strengthened finance capital and reinforced the concentration and centralization of production, thereby bringing the decisive strata of finance capital to supremacy in the fascist dictatorship.

Between 1923 and 1926, a number of changes arose having direct repercussions in political life. The supremacy of the decisive strata of finance capital, and the fact that they had broken all resistance, found correspondence at the political level in the political unification of the bourgeoisie on the most reactionary basis.

Totalitarianism was born. Fascism was not born totalitarian; it became so when the decisive strata of the bourgeoisie reached their maximum degree of economic, and therefore political, unification.

Totalitarianism is another concept that does not come from fascist ideology. If you look at fascism's initial conception of the relations between the citizen and the state, you will notice elements of anarchic liberalism: the protest against state intervention in private affairs, etc. Totalitarianism, instead, is a reflection of the intervening change and the predominance of finance capital.

We can only make passing mention of these political aspects of the problem. When examining how the problem of totalitarianism was posed, you must also see the problems that had been posed during the preceding period. The bourgeoisie modified its front; fascism had to modify its [front] too. This change marked the beginning of discussions, struggles and changes within the Fascist Party. Heated debates took place in the party and the fascist trade unions. In the party, the fight centered on the problem of the Fascist Party's functions and the relationship of the party to the state.

The fascist conception, the conception held by the extremist middle-level cadres, was that the party should prevail over the state organizations. The party must command: this was the position held by Farinacci,[12] who said the provincial party secretary must outrank the provincial prefect.

The Nationalists Federzoni and Rocco[13] had a different idea. They said the state must come first, then the party, which is subordinate to the former.

Mussolini juggled these two ideas. During the Matteotti period, he used Farinacci; but when the problem of totalitarianism was at hand, he went with Rocco, giving the definitive formula: Everything in the state, nothing against the state.

This process was completed when the new measures were

taken. The Fascist Party became a simple instrument of the state for nationalist propaganda, etc., for tying the petty and middle bourgeoisie to the state; for influencing the workers.

The problem of the trade unions was more important. How was it framed? Unfortunately, we can only outline it briefly. There was a 100 percent about-face on the trade-union question.

Take the figures regarding fascist trade-union membership. You can see they were negligible at the beginning. Back then, fascism *was not organizing but disorganizing* the masses. Between 1920 and 1923, the fascist trade unions organized several hundred thousand workers, but the workers who left the class unions could be counted in the millions. Fascism's scope in this period was to disorganize the workers.

This lasted until the Matteotti period. Fascism tried to organize the workers but did not succeed. But when the problem of totalitarianism arose, when fascism set out on the road to the totalitarian organization of the state, the front changed: fascism then had to organize the workers within the framework of its own trade unions; it no longer could limit itself to severing them from the class unions, but had to organize them on its own account.

How was this problem resolved? Here, too, there were a good many steps. The groundwork of the solution was the Law of 1926 which set up the trade-union monopoly, destroyed the shop committees, etc. Based on this trade-union monopoly, the would-be conquest of the masses began.

Bear in mind that a further modification came later. Totalitarianism in 1926, 1927, 1928 was not the same as totalitarianism in its 1931 version. This last modification was prompted by the change in the country's economic situation, by the crisis of the Italian economy.

When did this crisis begin? It began at the end of 1929 and the start of 1930. But we have always stressed that there were harbingers of the crisis as early as 1927; signs corresponding to a development of the economic contradictions caused by the growth of the productive apparatus, by industrial concentration, etc., by the whole technical and organizational development of capitalism. This development resulted at first in over capacity. Then, in 1926, the problem of cutting production costs made itself acutely felt, and the attack on wages thus became a necessity.

Thereafter, fascism would never stray from the path of totalitarianism. It had become a necessity. The struggle against the working class developed in full, continuing to this very day.

When the crisis assumed acute form at the end of 1929, the problem at hand had changed. It was no longer enough to disorganize the masses; something else was needed. The masses' alienation from the regime would have meant the shrinking of fascism's mass base. This problem grew extremely sharp.

Thus, the second aspect of fascist policy—mass policy—appeared on the scene. Mass policy is a necessity the economic situation and class relations imposed on the Italian bourgeoisie, in order to cope with the splits in its mass base and counter the growth of anti-fascist movements.

The situation apparently has remained stagnant from 1930 to today; but the problem is acute, and its acuteness is reflected in the numerous changes of position, changings of the guard, etc.

Of these changings of the guard, one was decisive: the liquidation of Rocco in mid-1932. It signified a change in the nature of fascist totalitarianism, marking the beginning of the so-called popular policy.

At present, fascism is making an enormous effort to bring the masses into its organizations, to keep them tied to the dictatorship's apparatus. These problems of the organization of the Fascist Party, of the youth, of the trade unions, are still being framed from a totalitarian viewpoint, but in a way that is just a little bit different.

What I have wanted to demonstrate in yesterday's and today's lesson is that fascism must not be viewed as something which is definitively characterized; that it must be seen in its development, never as something set, never as a scheme or model, but as the consequence of a series of real economic and political relations resulting from real factors—from the economic situation, from the struggle of the masses.

It is wrong to think totalitarianism bars the path of struggle to us. It is wrong to think totalitarianism closes the path of the fight for democratic gains to the masses. It is wrong. Fascism is attempting to lead us onto this ground. Fascism is trying to make us think that all is over; that we have entered a new period in which the only thing to do is to put ourselves on its ground.

The slightest concession to this point of view must be fought vigorously. Each development of the mass struggle reopens the problem of the fascist dictatorship. It would be enough to multiply the actual mass movements to provoke fresh modifications in the dictatorship. Fascism tends to change its front with every drive by the masses. This we have already seen.

The conception of fascism that I have been illustrating must underlie our entire policy. A correct policy line can be determined only on the basis of this conception.

Totalitarianism does not close the path of struggle to the Party but opens new paths.

We are wrong, we who are not always able to see quickly the new paths of struggle fascism opens to us.

This failing is one of analysis and of political incapacity. But insofar as the Party is able to understand this, it will succeed in reopening the question of the fascist dictatorship.

lecture 3

The National Fascist Party

I BELIEVE it won't be easy for the comrades to have a good understanding of the existence of the Fascist Party in the Italian situation, and of what it means today, if they don't refer to my previous exposition and especially to what I said about the situation with regard to the political organization of the forces of the bourgeoisie before fascism came to power or, rather, before the war.

The bourgeoisie had never possessed a strong, unified political organization; it never had an organization in party form. This was one of the characteristics of the Italian situation before the war. Before the war, you could not find a bourgeois political organization having the name, the character, of a political party; I mean a centralized national organization linked with the masses and having a definite program and line of action equal throughout the country. Make an effort to find one such organization; no use, you will not find it.

This political phenomenon was a direct consequence of the structure of the Italian economy. This political weakness was a consequence of the fact that big industry, while prevalent from a certain point of view, was not yet able to regulate the entire economic life of the nation. The agricultural economy still carried great weight in the Italian economy, and the intermediate strata, extremely numerous and playing a big role, also carried not inconsiderable weight.

For all you may look, you will not find in Italy a situation such as could be found in England, for example, where there were two typical parties—the Liberals and the Conservatives—which had a character of solidarity, a program, a policy line applied on the national scale, a compactness, and which succeeded one another in power. In Italy, none of this.

In Italy, instead, there was a whole series of parties and political groups that were unable to attain the shape of a national party expressing a whole current of bourgeois opinion. The prewar parliament had within it the representatives of a great number of parties and groups.

But if you look at the political and organizational solidity of these parties and groups, you will reach the same conclusions: the dividing lines are not sharply drawn, they are blurred; and the more you move toward the larger groups, the more the party nature is lost. The most numerous group was the Giolittians, but even it was not a political party. Every deputy was elected in his own locality by a group which, as an organization, never went beyond its own region. In Turin, for example, we have the Liberal Monarchist Union. These clusters were not such as to permit the formation of a solidly organized party.

You will find something different, instead, going toward the Left, going toward organizations which gathered the working masses. Here you will find the party.

The most solid bourgeois party in the prewar Chamber of Deputies was the Radical Party. Why? Because its rank-and-file base was in large part to be found in the working masses of the North. The Radical Party was a party that arose on the same terrain as the Socialist Party and then deviated toward the line of bourgeois democracy. But the period of its formation was characterized by the struggle for strata of the proletariat, and for this it already took the shape of a party.

The only party in the prewar period, the only real party, was the Socialist Party. The Socialist Party was the only party that could have run the same candidate in elections in Milan and Cagliari. The designation of the same Liberal candidate in Turin and Bari, for example, would have been inconceivable.

The bloc of bourgeois forces was built, back then, through a whole series of parliamentary and extra-parliamentary compromises. This is true of the period that goes from 1890 to 1898, for example, and of the Giolittian period.

Furthermore, you will find a very marked difference between the bourgeois political groups of the North and those of the South. In the North, you will find rather far-reaching political groups, you will find the tendency toward the formation of a liberal party. The question of unifying the bourgeois forces was being posed and was being discussed in the press, although it was not settled at the time.

Go down South, instead. There, you won't find even this. There, the organization of the bourgeoisie was even more fragmented on the basis of local and even personal interests. The Radical Party, the Socialist Party, the Republican Party (which, as we shall see, no longer was a party in the true sense of the word, but a remnant, without a national character, which had bases only in a few localities) took on a marked local stamp in the South. Look, for example, at the Socialist Party. The history of the Socialist Party in Naples was not the same as in the other regions of Italy. In certain respects, it resembled the other bourgeois organizations. This resemblance could be seen in the struggles among groups, in personal intrigues, etc. The same thing happened in Sicily. There, organized dissidence took a particular form, so much so that it even went as far as to form a party. At the time of the reformist schism of Reggio Emilia,[1] the "Sicilian" Reformist Party had some rank-and-file formations which split off, existing for a certain length of time as separate organizations in Messina, Catania, etc.

The Italian bourgeoisie did have one unified political organization which, however, was not a political party: the Freemasonry. Before the war, the Freemasonry was the only unitary political organization of the bourgeoisie. It played a role of prime importance not only in the struggle for the unification of the Italian state, not only in the fight for Italy's national liberation, but also in the process of the political unification of the Italian bourgeoisie's various groups and in the consolidation of the big bourgeoisie's influence over the petty and middle bourgeoisie. As far as I know, there are no figures on the composition of the Freemasonry in this period. But if such figures did exist, they would indicate a large percentage of petty-bourgeois and salaried employees. Pay attention to this fact, for you will find the exact same traits later on in the National Fascist Party. The petty bourgeoisie joined the Freemasonry as an organization which defended its interests in a society in which legality was not something that could be relied on, and in which the breaking of this legality was frequent both by the governors and by the governed. It was a kind of mutual-aid society. Salaried employees joined it in order to advance their careers, and some went on to become high dignitaries. But the agricultural bourgeoisie and the industrialists also were in the Freemasonry. For the bourgeoisie, it represented the organization with the most extensive and unitary structure in prewar Italian society.

Two large parties appeared on the political scene in the postwar period. The Socialist Party, which had existed before the war and which several months before the outbreak of the war had severed its ties with the bourgeoisie (in point of fact, its break with the Freemasonry came just a few months before the war); an autonomous, independent party with a class character and spread throughout Italy. And at the same time we have the Popular Party.[2]

The Popular Party was a new phenomenon in Italian society in that it represented the organization, the political party, of the urban and rural petty-bourgeois strata, of the peasants, of strata which up to then had formed the base of all the political parties. Up to then, all the parties had had their bases in these urban and rural petty-bourgeois strata.

The Popular Party, with its particular program, was organized autonomously on a sectarian basis. In the intentions of the Catholic Church, the Popular Party should have been—and was in fact—an organization designed to slow the Socialist Party's advance. This objective was reached. But, at the same time, it tended to break up, and in part did break up, the Italian bourgeoisie's traditional structures of political rule. This is one of the phenomena that would heighten the postwar crisis.

Hence, the problem the bourgeoisie posed itself after the war was that of creating its own autonomous organization.

Orginally, the Fascist Party did not set itself this task. It set itself this task and followed through with it in the course of the struggle against the workers to establish the dictatorship of the most reactionary strata of the bourgeoisie, and in the course of the fight to strengthen this dictatorship.

We already have seen what the Fascist Party was originally.

Let's take the Fascist Party in the first period of its existence, before and immediatley after it took power. There are statistics on Fascist Party membership at the time of the 3rd Congress, the Rome Congress held at the Augusteo. These statistics cover 151 thousand members: this was the number of party members. Of these 151 thousand, 14 thousand were merchants (note that the designation merchant covered all kinds of people—they were the rich), 4 thousand were industrialists, 18 thousand landowners, 21 thousand students and teachers, 10 thousand professional men, 7 thousand public officials, 15 thousand salaried employees, 25 thousand factory workers and seamen, 27 thousand agricultural workers.

If you study these figures, which must be taken with a grain of salt but which still are indicative of something, you will see that the highest figure in absolute terms is the one for agricultural workers. These agricultural workers came mostly from Emilia, from strata of the rural petty and middle bourgeoisie which in fascism's first period had constituted its principal mass base.

But if we take the industrialists, merchants, landowners, students (in reality, the sons of the former) and professional men, we have 67 thousand members, that is to say half the total number. Then we have 22 thousand salaried employees and public officials, a rather large number as you can see. We have 25 thousand industrial workers and seamen: this is the most questionable figure. Nonetheless, assuming it to be true, we can see that in overall percentage terms it was not these 25 thousand who determined the party's nature. The party's nature was given by the 67 thousand bourgeois and 22 thousand salaried employees. *The Fascist Party was a predominantly bourgeois party with strong influence on the salaried employees and with offshoots in the working class and among the agricultural workers.*

This was the character of the Fascist Party before it took power, when it still bore the original imprint of the petty-and middle-bourgeois masses, when it still was raising issues with revolutionary tendencies, when the original program of the *fasci di combattimento* had not yet been completely set aside, when the Fascist Party's transformation into the assault force of the bourgeoisie was still under way.

When the Fascist Party took power, it set itself a dual objective. The first objective, posed gradually, not all at once, was to destroy all the other parties of the Italian bourgeoisie and all political parties in general. This objective was not posed at the outset, but took shape in the course of the development of the fascist dictatorship, in the course of the struggle to overcome the political and economic difficulties which arose.

The Fascist Party began by trying to establish alliances with the other parties of the Italian bourgeoisie. In 1921, before coming to power, the Fascist Party had presented itself to the voters as an ally of various other political parties of the bourgeoisie. In the 1924 elections, even after it had come to power and despite the fact the elections were held under fascist control, the Fascist Party did not run a pure Fascist slate but one on which, together with the fascist elements, there were representatives of a series of old political parites of the Italian bourgeoisie, from the old conservatives and old liberals to the Giolittians and to Giolitti himself a candidate, if I am not mistaken, on the same local slate as Mussolini.

You see what the Fascist Party's stance was. In 1921, it had only thirty deputies despite the fact it had taken part in the elections in alliance with other parties. In 1924, it won a strong majority: two-thirds. It accomplished this by means of the new election law giving two-thirds of the seats to those with half the popular vote, and by means of the bloc formed with the old liberal and conservative parties of the Italian bourgeoisie. In this period, something of the old Giolittian method remained in the line taken toward the other political formations of the Italian bourgeoisie.

But the problem of destroying the other political parties arose immediately, in 1923, '24, '25. The Fascist Party first assaulted those parties whose mass bases resembled fascism's original mass base. Thus, it assailed the Popular Party before the Reformist Party, and the Reformist Party before the Communist

Party. Why? The struggle was waged more fiercely against the Popular and Reformist parties than against us in that period because those parties' mass bases were akin to the original mass base of fascism: they reached into petty- and middle-bourgeois strata, peasant strata; they reached into the same strata that fascism wanted to have in its own ranks so as to be a mass party. Sharp competition developed, expressed in a particularly intense political struggle, to win over or retain these mass strata.

The program of destroying other parties steadily expanded and finally led to the laws of 1925-26 outlawing the old political parties. On top of that, these laws also were the signal for the offensive to destroy what in the prewar period had been the Italian bourgeoisie's only unitary organization: the Freemasonry.

Fascism turned on the Freemasonry relatively late—in 1925—but the struggle was extremely swift and was carried straight to its ultimate consequences. The Fascist Party couldn't tolerate the existence of the Freemasonry; it couldn't tolerate it since the Fascist Party's aim was to become the only party of the Italian bourgeoisie. This problem of becoming the only party was raised particularly in 1925 and 1926. From that moment on, the Freemasonry was tolerated no longer; its death bell tolled. All the other political parties had to disappear.

Fascism's political plan broadened at this time. We thus reach the second stage of its evolution. The mere destruction of the parties that opposed the open dictatorship of the most reactionary strata of the bourgeoisie no longer was enough; the Fascist Party also had to assimilate the cadres of these parties into its own ranks and thereby realize unity among the ruling classes from the organizational standpoint as well.

You will find an index of this situation on p. 25 of the material, where you can see when the old political parties were destroyed and absorbed by the Fascist Party. In 1920 and 1922 we have most of the Republicans of Romagna and Emilia, and the Mazzinian groups outside the Republican Party. In May 1923 we have the merger with the Nationalist Party. This merger's value was twofold. On the one hand it meant that the most reactionary groups of the bourgeoisie unreservedly accepted the Fascist Party's hegemony from the organizational point of view, but at the same time it changed the Fascist Party's course of development. You will begin to find profound modifications in the Fascist Party at this time. What was said of Greece and Rome can be said of these two parties. The Nationalist Party was a small affair before the merger. In some places, the Nationalists had even been treated roughly by the Fascists. Thus, they had been conquered. But afterward they became conquerors.

This is something of the utmost importance to an understanding of the character of the fascist dictatorship. It's no coincidence that Rocco, a Nationalist, has been the lawgiver of this dictatorship; it's no coincidence that Bottai,[3] another Nationalist, has been one of its leading figures. In every stage, a struggle has been waged between Fascists and Nationalists to solve the fundamental problems of the state and of the party. The substance of the solution to these problems has always come from the Nationalist Party; the substance of their solution has always been clearly reactionary and bourgeois.

The third stage was characterized by the disbanding of the associations of Italian democracy—Nittian democracy, liberal democracy, radicals, social democracy, Freemasonry of the Scottish rite, etc. Today you will find that the representatives, the survivors of these pulverized Italian democracies, of these democracies that existed in the prewar years, have been installed in the leading positions in the Italian economy. The Italian economy's most authoritative name is Beneduce,[4] a leader of one of these parties. Others like him occupy decisive posts in the Italian economy.

In 1923 the maximalists of the Gironde, whose head was Cesare Alessandri,[5] attached themselves to the Fascist Party. In August of 1924 it was the turn of the center of the Popular Party, which had stayed alive though it had not only flanked fascism but had become completely fascist. In the summer of '22 and in October of '25 it was the turn of the right-wing Liberals, from Salandra[6] to the right wing of Giolitti's party. Finally, in 1927 we have Rigola and company,[7] who, however, did not actually join the Fascist Party but fastened themselves to it in a certain way.

What has been said so far shows the process of the destruction of the old organizations and the assimilation of the old cadres. It was in this moment that the problem sharpened; it was in this moment that the party's crises began. Why?

Briefly, on the crises of the Fascist Party.

They originated primarily in the conflicts within the Italian petty and middle bourgeoisie, fascist-organized masses which had been opposed originally to the establishment of the open dictatorship of the most reactionary strata of the bourgeoisie.

The crises of Italian fascism should not be confused with the crises of other movements—of German fascism, for example. There, the discontent of the middle strata, of the unemployed, etc., has a much larger role. In Italy, the crises did not have this character; the working masses weren't in the Fascist Party back then.

The ones who set themselves against the party were the petty-bourgeois heads of the local Fascist party organizations and the petty-bourgeois masses of the countryside, who felt the pressure of the fascist dictatorship to an intolerable degree; hence the discontent, the split in all of fascism's local organizations after the March on Rome.

You can find information on this in an article by our ex-comrade Pasquini[8] examining the crises of 1925-27.

What was Forni, for example? A typical angry petty bourgeois of the postwar period, one who was paid by the rural capitalists but who nevertheless imagined he had a major role in Italian political life. The same goes for Sala, Misuri, etc.[9] In every fascist organization there was a type of dissident leader who plotted revolt, tended to rebel and provoked crises.

All did not do so, however. A great many were absorbed into the state apparatus, into the economic apparatus of the bourgeoisie. In 1923, the Fascists surged onto the lists of members of the boards of directors of the major corporations, especially of those, such as the insurance companies, that do not have decisive guiding functions.

There was a whole series of famous scandals, the origins of which should be sought in this invasion of Fascists, who through theft, fraud, etc. tried to become capitalists, to play a leading role in the field of the economy. This is important because it reflects, paradoxically, the transformation of the Fascist Party into the party of the Italian big bourgeoisie.

Fascism had to put an end to this rebelliousness if it wanted to solve the problem of being a unitary party. So Mussolini clearly set this task: to change the Fascist Party's cadres. It was at this time that Mussolini formulated this concept: the Fascist Party cannot hold power with the same cadres with which it seized it.

The struggle against the old cadres was not an easy or uniform process. These cadres were tied to groups, to the rank and file. If we analyze the composition of the Fascist Party leadership, we have to wait until 1927 to see a real change of cadres. They no longer were the 1919'ers, but rural capitalists, industrialists, student sons of capitalists, etc.; or Fascists who had become leaders in the economic structure of the bourgeoisie. This process, therefore, was brought near to completion in 1927. But the problem had been very grave, and an acute struggle had been waged over it in the Fascist Party. From the ideological standpoint, this struggle centered on the issue of the party's role; from the organizational standpoint, on the issue of who ought to lead it.

The most interesting point concerning the first issue—the definition of the Fascist Party and its position in relation to the state—is that we can see in it, as the outcome of the process, a completely different conception from the one that had been the point of departure.

Mussolini started out with the conception of the Fascist Party as a *movement*. This meant in itself that the party had to be dominant, that it had to be all-encompassing. This had been Mussolini's original conception. But this conception was abandoned at the Congress at the Augusteo.

Later, you can clearly see two positions: the party as the predominant element, this being the position of the old petty-bourgeois cadres, of Farinacci; and the other position, according to which the party should be subordinate to the state, upheld by the old conservative elements of the Nationalist Party, by Federzoni and Rocco. There were continual oscillations between these two positions from 1923 to 1932. What was the final outcome? You will find it in the Statute of the National Fascist Party, which you will read, not wasting time with details (seeing how a squad is organized, etc.), but dwelling on its political importance.

Article One states that the PNF is a civilian militia in the service of the state. What does this mean? It means that just when the party's existence is affirmed, it is negated: the party no longer is a party, it is a militia; what's more, a militia in the service of the state. Therefore it is the state that predominates.

There had been sharp clashes between party and state. The state was personified by the provincial prefect, the Fascist Party by the provincial party secretary. In 1923 this struggle had broken down the whole apparatus. The party secretary wanted to command the prefect. Various paths were taken to attenuate these crises: fascist prefects were designated, etc.

The most acute moment of crisis in this struggle came in 1924 and '25. Fascism reached the very brink of defeat in that moment. At a certain point, it was about to lose power. Pay attention to how it had to change its organizational formula at this time. The process of the party's assimilation into the state had to be suspended. The old cadres returned. Farinacci saved fascism in '24. Mussolini made a whole series of speeches in '24—from the speech in the Senate on down to January 3[10]—but these would have been to no avail if they had not been backed up by the action Farinacci conducted throughout Italy on the basis of the old ideology, on the basis of a return to the party's original forms.

We have seen, therefore, how the Fascist Party effected changes of front, and how the issues of relations between party and state, and of the organizing of the Fascist Party's dominion, were posed.

As we have seen, one of the critical points was 1925. Fascism was saved by Farinacci, by old cadres. This detail is noteworthy; it should be borne in mind. If you look closely, you will see that every time an acute political situation arises, every time the mass movements tend to broaden, fascism immediately leans towards maneuvers of this kind.

Thus, in 1932-33 the youth problem arose, the mass movements grew, the influence of our Communist Party increased, and fascism called out the old cadres.

Today, however, the cadre problem is not the same as it was in 1924 for the Fascist Party. It's not so dangerous anymore. The Fascist Party has grown stronger and is solidly welded to the state. The old petty-bourgeois ideology basically has been liquidated in it. Today, the old cadres, in part, have fallen, been eliminated, thrown into prison and interned. Sometimes they reappear as provocateurs among the emigrants, or they may be utilized by the Fascist Party, but they no longer have any policy-making function. The discussion on the definition of the party and its relationship to the state is not so acute anymore.

Today, the accepted formula, approved in '32, represents relations which exist de facto in the country; but its realization cost the Fascist Party a series of internal crises, a series of conflicts, of eliminations of men, of changings of the guard, etc.

It can be said that this transformation was effected in 1927. The decisive elements of the bourgeoisie were part of the Fascist Party organization; there already was a great mass of salaried employees and public officials in the Fascist Party; the factory workers and farm workers were still represented to a very small degree. This was the situation in 1927.

Thus, the problem of the Fascist Party's relationship to the state was about to be resolved; it was heading toward solution. The Fascist Party's internal structure was being changed.

In effect, the Fascist Party stopped being a party. Here you can see its dialectic development; it changed slowly from one position to the other, passing to a higher level. The Fascist Party stopped being a party. All discussion came to an end in it.

Political discussions do not exist. When the Fascist Party makes a change in its policy, its members read about it in the newspapers just like any other citizen. In no measure do they participate in determining its policy. Every form of internal democracy is lost. The party is organized from above along bureaucratic lines.

At the top is the Directorate elected by the Grand Council of Fascism, which isn't even a party organization but a state organization in which you will find the representatives of the party, state, banks, industry, etc. The Grand Council of Fascism is the organizational characteristic of the leading groups of the Italian bourgeoisie tied to fascism.

The Directorate's power stems from there; from the Directorate, it filters down to the local directorates and on down to the heads of the rank-and-file fascist formations.

It might be said that the Fascist Party's inner life is dead. Formally, a general membership meeting is held once a year, with the members listening to a series of solemn speeches. They approve the work of the old Directorate and ratify the new one. But this is a mere ratification, a formality which has nothing to do with elections of a democratic kind.

Nonetheless, it would be a mistake to believe that there is no inner life in the Fascist Party. Why? Because among the Fascist Party cadres, especially the middle-level cadres, the ones in contact with the rank and file, there are individuals who cannot keep from thinking, from judging the situation. They are affected by the influence of the masses with which they are in daily contact.

It is from these cadres that political reactions come. By what route, in what way? In a paradoxical way. These reactions are seen only when they reach their highest point. Look at the Arpinati case in Bologna,[11] for instance. It surfaced only when fascism could tolerate it no longer, when this group presented itself in relation to fascism with another program, with a program different from the official one.

This process goes on unobserved. It is more visible perhaps in the Fascist Party organizations in the countryside, where mass discontent is greatest, where the fascist organizations are tied more closely to the masses, where the helping hand of the police isn't as strong as in the cities. This explains the reason for the most recent large-scale phenomenon of rebelliousness in Emilia, where the disgruntlement of the masses is greatest.

This last phenomenon came in 1933-34, when for a year fascism had to make an exception to its general rule of recruitment. Recruitment is carried out through the annual fascist call-up; this is the normal way. Only in certain moments are the doors of the party thrown open. Today, they are closed. In 1933-34, membership was opened and a big effort was made to bring the workers in.

This campaign yielded results, it cannot be denied. The number of members increased by about 700-800 thousand.

There already had been isolated instances of workers joining the Fascist Party at FIAT, for example, and in some other factories at the start of 1932. But the big leap in membership was made in '34. From 1,099,000 at the start of the year, the members became 1,850,000 by the end of the year, increasing by roughly 800 thousand, including no doubt, a mass of factory workers.

A consequence of this injection of new forces has been the tightening of the bureaucratizing norms; the mass must not speak. But it has had another consequence: the existence of certain forms of political life on the fringes of the Fascist Party—something that is felt more strongly in the countryside than in the cities.

We haven't reached the end of this development. We have before us a Fascist Party with 1,800,000 members that embraces imposing strata of the Italian population and the whole Italian bourgeoisie. No other political organization of the Italian bourgeoisie exists today. With very rare exceptions, there is not one bourgeois who is not a member of the Fascist Party. The bourgeoisie's old political forms have been liquidated for good.

This is an element of strength for the bourgeoisie. Although the party loses the character of a party, it unifies to a large measure the ideology of the Italian bourgeoisie. And this gives the bourgeoisie an element of strength. This must not be forgotten; it is of very great importance.

In the Fascist Party the Italian bourgeoisie has a new type of political organization, one fit to exercise open dictatorship on the working classes. What's more, through a whole series of other structures and ties, the Fascist Party has become an organization that has given the Italian bourgeoisie the capability of exerting armed pressure on the working masses at all times. Parallel to itself, in fact, the Fascist Party has created a Militia which also has undergone transformations, but which, in spite of everything, has preserved its character as an armed party organization. The Militia is not the same thing as the *Carabinieri* corps or the Army, although it has taken something from the latter. Through the Militia, the party controls vast strata of the masses. It is one of the chief bases of the dictatorship's strength.

Here, too, there have been contradictions. But the absence of political life makes it difficult to give the Militia a certain solidity, a compactness; and, as we will see later, this offers us a chance to carry on a certain kind of work in it. However, it would be a mistake not to see these contradictions and not to see that the Fascist Party represents an element of strength.

At bottom, membership in the Fascist Party represents a bond—a more or less large ideological bond, and an organizational bond. In a certain sense, it can be said that the workers who have joined the party have been made to wear a kind of military uniform. The soldier, too, is unhappy with his situation, but he is a soldier, has a uniform, submits, obeys and cannot rebel except in the event of a revolutionary crisis.

These bonds can be cut only with tenacious work by our Party. It is an error to think these bonds will break by themselves. Some of the resistance we run up against in our work at the base, in the factories, is due, perhaps, to the fact that we do not always understand how this bond must be cut. We do not always know how to adapt our slogans and limit the objectives for workers who are made to wear this kind of uniform. We do not always know how to interpret their state of mind and the path by which they can be led into the struggle.

This is an element that must be kept in mind in the practical application of our tactic of exploiting the legal possibilities.

lecture 4

Fascism's Military and Propaganda Organizations

TO DATE, we have spoken of the formation and development of the Fascist Party; we have described the type of organization and the political character of the activity of the Fascist Party, as it has been set and consolidated since the promulgation of its new statute.

We have stressed how the characteristic element is the absence of all forms of internal democracy, the lack of debate, the absence of any real political life. We have seen how its character is that of a *civilian militia;* how there are no elections to party posts; how, in a word, it has a particularly bureaucratic character corresponding to the character of the dictatorship, which liquidated the democratic institutions and revealed itself as an open dictatorship. The Fascist Party's character corresponds to this feature of the dictatorship: the liquidation of every form of democracy.

This is why there is something true in Mussolini's statement, copied from Lenin, that he has created a *new type* of party. This element—the liquidation of every form of democracy, the party's adaptation to the forms of the dictatorship—really does give the party some new traits.

We must always remember, however, that this party's organizational forms are not something stable, but have been shaped in the course of the party's development, and have not been foreseen by Mussolini.

An immediate consequence of the way the Fascist Party is organized and of its influence on the life of the nation is that the struggles, the inevitable contradictions which in a democratic regime would have found expression in the fight among various parties, are brought into the party itself.

Today, we shall examine a series of fascist organizations.

Could the Fascist Party, as presently organized, exert control on the entire life of the nation and on all the strata of the population? Obviously not, due to its excessive bureaucratization and that purely outer homogeneity which makes it barren, which leaves it without a line in adapting itself to the needs of all the strata.

What does it mean to be a member of the Fascist Party in Italy today? Some of the members are politically active, hold office, exercise a political function. But if you think of the great number of members, you will see that the vast majority of them are politically passive. Despite this, they still belong to the party. Why? Because they are obliged to join by a whole series of constraints. These constraints are twofold in nature: direct and indirect. Indirect constraints are represented by the fact, for example, that membership in the Fascist Party is a prerequisite for holding any civil service job; that membership in the Fascist Party is an absolute requisite for gaining entrance to competitive civil service examinations; that you can't be a clerk, teacher or university professor in Italy today if you aren't a party member. The sphere widens when you consider that this kind of constraint extends to all the free professions: lawyers, journalists, etc., must be party members. Doctors, the ones who enjoyed the most freedom in the past, also have been subjected to this form of constraint. You can't be a Public Health doctor today without joining the Fascist Party.

In this way, you can see what an enormous mass of petty and middle bourgeois join the Fascist Party since they work, since they must live, and to live they must work.

Another form of constraint is the open constraint used in the factories on the workers. True, it has not yet been established that if you want to continue to work, you must be a member; but, for example, in hiring, of two unemployed—one a party member, the other not—the Fascist gets the preference. Thus, among the workers, too, there has been a certain modification of the traditional earlier relations. It's true, there is an element in common in that labor-power still is being sold, and is being bought by the bosses; but elements of political organizations are penetrating these traditional relations today.

Given this form of constraint, when you are dealing with members of the Fascist Party not only do you see them politically inactive, not engaged in politics, but you can see how these individuals are bound to fascism by rather tenuous ties. A regional [PCI] leader told us in one of his reports that one day he had come across an employee of a large cooperative-style commercial association who was crying. This happened in a big industrial city. What's the matter? asked our comrade. And the man replied that he was desperate because he had to pay forty lire to join the [Fascist] party. And so why are you joining? He answered that he had to join if he wanted to keep from being fired with the first cutback of personnel. But then you are not a Fascist? Fascist?! The devil take the Fascists!

Here we have this individual. How can he be an active member? His ties to the Fascist Party organization are exclusively economic. He is a Fascist only because he must support his family. The political ties are quite tenuous.

If you generalize this case, you'll see that things are like this everywhere. If you look at the overall picture, you'll see how fascism must create other organizations if it wants to control the masses. Why? Because if it doesn't create these organizations, these strata will escape it or will activate the Fascist Party. And the Fascist Party, for its very characteristics, cannot be activated without endangering fascism itself.

If you compare the activity of the members of the Fascist Party to the activity of the members of a parallel organization, for example the members of the *Opera Balilla,* [1] you will see that the *Balilla* is more active than the Fascist. The same fact strikes the eye for all the parallel organizations. What we have is a large party organization with a great mass in which there is only a small active nucleus. This nucleus serves to organize the mass on the basis of particular interests, adapting its forms of organization to the concrete objectives that fascism aims to reach.

The whole series of fascist organizations can be divided into three types: military, propaganda-military and trade-union. The difference among these three types is not very marked. We can take the Militia as characteristic of the first type, the Young Fascists for the second, and the fascist unions for the third. These organizations have some points in common. For example, the premilitary training groups have something in common with both the Militia and the Youth Fascists, the civil service associations (clerks, railwaymen, etc.) resemble the trade unions but are not trade unions.

Let's examine some of these organizations.

Let's start with the Militia. We have a good deal in our material, but not everything we need. It would be good if someone found more. If possible, it would be good to find the statute of the Militia.

The material we have available to us does not show two fundamental things: the transformation of the Militia from fascism's rise to power up to today; and the transformation of its internal stratification, not with regard to the social classes to which militiamen belong, but in relation to their duties, to their military obligations. Today, the Militia has a basic nucleus with a ten-year term of service. This is a characteristic element. It did not exist before. Before, the Militia was an organization of *squadristi*. It took time to reach the present point. Fascism initially had wanted to make use of the Militia in the form of *squadrismo* (not as an army) in actions for which the state did not want to assume responsibility. The Militia started to take its present form when totalitarianism began to be organized in all branches.

Today, the Militia has a nucleus of professional soldiers. It has a dual function: it acts as a political police in the broadest sense of the word—not only strictly as a police, but as an instrument to be used for social repression. At this point, an observation must be made: in recent years, fascism has tended to use the Militia only in extreme cases; it makes use exclusively of the police and *carabinieri* to handle small-scale movements. This tendency reveals a certain distrust. It's easy to understand the class character of today's economic conflicts; even simple peasants can understand it. This is the reason why quite a few times the militiamen have not marched against peasants in revolt, have gone over to their side, have struck a stance of sympathy for the struggle against the bosses. But there is another element to this tendency: the Militia is being trained to intervene in social movements of a vaster nature, to intervene in civil war. It is being given real training for this purpose. It is being prepared to smother vast mass movements, not small scale local conflicts. Its function can be compared with that of the Army, but with the addition of the political discipline imposed on it. The Militia today is trained to employ all the weapons that are used in civil war: rifles, machine guns, tanks, etc. What's more, it is also being trained to use airplanes, radio, gases, etc. And at the same time it is undergoing political indoctrination.

Its second function is related to the Italian military establishment. The Militia forms cadres of future officers. Its function is analogous to the one fulfilled in disarmed Germany by the Reichswehr, which is training 100 thousand men as professional soldiers. The tendency is to make the Militia a corps which, when necessary, can regiment the masses. This is why, when considering the armed forces of Italy, one cannot limit oneself to the Army with its term of service, etc. Fascism can also reduce the term of compulsory service. It is able to set up a type of military organization different from the traditional one of the other states of the Continent; different from the French one, for example. Fascism's military organization is based on the existence of ready-trained cadres and on mass militarization. The Militia is one of the pivotal points of the plan for achieving this kind of organization.

We should remember that the Militia's social structure comes very close to that of the Army. Of great importance is the fact that the Militia no longer is the same thing as the old-style squads led by the rural capitalists, etc. Groups of unemployed are brought into it just as is done in France, for example, with the volunteer formations of the Army. This fact is of great importance because it opens up to us possibilities of work in the Militia akin to the ones we have in the Army.

We come now, to the organizations that are not only military but propagandistic: *Balilla,* Youth Vanguards, Young Fascists. The *Balilla* formations hold children up to age fourteen. The Youth Vanguards at first organized youths up to the point they joined the Fascist Party, but then a division was introduced between Vanguardists and Young Fascists. The Vanguardists go up to age seventeen, while the Young Fascists go from age seventeen up to the point of membership in the Fascist Party.

This organization, too, was not created all at once; it was formed through a whole series of attempts, of experiments.

The *Balilla* organization was voluntary in nature until 1926-27. Then it became compulsory; but not one-hundred percent compulsory, just ninety percent compulsory. Parents were forced to register their children in the *Balilla*. If this obligation was transgressed, there would be fines, etc.

The general rule was: mandatory registration.

There is a big difference between this organization and the Fascist party organization; the obligatory nature is much more accentuated in the former than the latter. Strictly speaking, the factory worker is not obliged to join the Fascist Party. His son who attends school must join the *Balilla.* Here we have the obligatory nature of this organization. The same is true of the Youth Vanguards; although somewhat looser, the obligatory nature is present here, too. If we then turn to the Young Fascists, we can see how the obligatory nature is present and takes specific forms. And it is precisely on the Young Fascists that I would like to dwell longest in order to demonstrate the difference between these mass organizations and the Fascist Party.

What are the duties of a Fascist Party member? What is he bound to do? Aside from the general obligations, such as loving the nation, serving the fatherland, etc., he is required to do very little: to attend the general membership meeting once a year, to take part in some parades, to frequent the neighborhood club. In reality, not even this frequentation is mandatory.

The Young Fascists, instead, first of all have a uniform they must buy and wear regularly. They have frequent mobilizations—almost every Sunday—military instruction, etc. Furthermore, the Young Fascists have a military-style regimentation that embraces the entire membership. The squad-leader is permanently in contact with all the youths. There is a hierarchy going from the upper units on down to the last member. This doesn't exist in the Fascist Party. The Young Fascist knows every day who his squad-leader is; he knows the squad-leader can call on him at his home at any moment. He must go to camp (fifty fascist youth camps were organized last year); this is another obligation the Fascists do not have.

Looking at the obligations, you will find they are much larger in this parallel mass organization than in the Fascist Party. This is the first feature of this organization.

The second feature is represented by the fact that, despite these larger obligations, it has a more marked mass character than the Fascist Party. Look at the current figure for the members of the *Balilla*: there are more than one million, almost as many as in the party. In 1930 there were already 1,300,000, while the party barely counted one million. If you bear in mind that the *Balilla* organization covers the population within certain age limits, that is to say from six to fourteen years of age, whereas the Fascist Party covers a much larger part, this mass character will stand out even more clearly. The same goes for the Young Fascists. From the day they were created, the Young Fascists have fluctuated around the half-million mark, and yet they only cover a few years—from eighteen to twenty-one. If you contrast this to the mass of the adult population covered by the Fascist Party, their mass character will stand out even more clearly. And in spite of this, their obligations are greater. There's an apparent contradiction in this. How is it resolved? It is resolved through greater constraint.

We have already spoken about the *Balilla*. Now let's see about the Young Fascists. They were created in a critical moment for the organization of the fascist dictatorship, in 1930. At that time, the crisis was beginning, the militancy of the masses was rising, the work of the Communist Party was being stepped up, while the problem of the Catholic Youth[2] still had not been solved.

It was in 1930 that the Fascist Party posed the problem of tying up the young people who were coming out of the Youth Vanguards but not entering the Fascist Party. The Fascist Party did not have a political life. Young people could not be tied up as in other organizations. There was a gap between the time youths reached age eighteen and the time they joined the Fascist Party. The Fascist Party intended to fill this gap by creating the Young Fascists.

When this organization arose it counted 380 thousand members, in 1931 it jumped to 800 thousand (the fight against the Catholic organizations), in 1932 it fell by a half-million, that is to say it lost about half its members. Nineteen thirty two was a year of particularly numerous struggles, the year of the Communist Party's growth, the year in which the Young Catholics grew even more than the Young Fascists shrank. Finally, it was the year in which many Young Fascists came over to us, to our Youth Federation; it was the year of our big organizing in Emilia, Tuscany, etc.

So fascism then loosed the reaction against us and against the Catholics. The Young Fascist organization gained 350 thousand members, but fell back again to 450 thousand in 1933.

These oscillations are due in part to the constraint used in recruitment. Young people have no trade. The factories are closed. Their only prospect is that of remaining unemployed. The students coming out of the universities find everything closed to them. This forms an uncertain, hesitant, vacillating mass easily penetrated by revolutionary ideology. Fascism endeavors to impede this penetration.

We have different reports on the problem of enrollment in the Young Fascists. In some regions, enrollment is voluntary; in others, it is mandatory. Evidently, a difference exists. But upon obtaining a general picture, we have seen that it is not possible to make any comparison between the pressures used to make the youth join the Young Fascists and those used to make adults join the party. Young people can't be told: if you don't join, you won't get a job! Young people won't find jobs all the same. This threat wouldn't frighten them.

They are made to resolve the problem of membership "voluntarily," by means of bureaucratic pressure, and there is no reluctance to employ violence as well. We can see, therefore, how the Young Fascists are more tied up in various projects, are more compelled to join than the members of the other organizations, have the most obligations and constraints. If these things are not borne in mind, then our Youth Federation's policy toward the

Young Fascists cannot be understood. It is precisely because of this character of the Young Fascists that our Youth Federation's policy toward them is particularly bold and audacious.

Let's look at the premilitary training groups. The premilitary training groups were at first a state organization, directly attached to the Army, rather than a party organization. It was almost completely voluntary. There was some constraint, which consisted in the fact that those who had taken the courses obtained certain advantages, such as reduction of the term of service, assignment to special corps and to certain localities, etc. All this somewhat diminished its voluntary nature.

The premilitary groups were transformed into a compulsory organization by a state law and placed under the immediate control of the Fascist Party, which through this organization exercises a direct influence on youths. In creating the Young Fascists organization, fascism did not suppress the premilitary groups; it retrained them. It knows the youth problem is a difficult one and can be solved more easily with two organizations than with one. A good deal can be accomplished with the premilitary training groups, but not everything. The same goes for the Young Fascists, which,as we have seen, are particularly subject to large fluctuations in their membership. The premilitary training groups must help the Young Fascists and, vice versa, the Young Fascists must sustain the premilitary training groups.

The final feature of these organizations is that their leadership is formed by active nuclei from the Fascist Party. You have interesting figures in this regard. Fascism employs about 50 thousand Fascists to direct the youth organizations politically and militarily. Reckoning that there are about a half-million Young Fascists, you can see that there is one adult leader for every ten youths. This active nucleus, these instructors in many cases are militiamen, frequently Fascists are paid specially for this work. The active nucleus of the Fascist Party represents the connective tissue of the whole regime.

Another form of bond between the Fascist Party and these organizations is the organizational bond that comes from the bureaucracy's direction of the youth formations. You know that until a short time ago the Young Fascists had to be *controlled* by the provincial party secretaries. Now it has been decided that the provincial party secretaries must *direct* the Young Fascists. This is repeated throughout the hierarchy: the party secretary is commandant of the Young Fascists, etc. The party's immediate direction of the Young Fascists is exercised in this way.

This is another way the Fascists admit that the Young Fascists represent one of the most important problems of fascism, one of the most critical points.

Before coming to the trade unions, we shall also say a few words about the Fascist University Groups. They have 60 thousand young people in their ranks, all of them elements of the petty and middle bourgeoisie. We should also recall the fascist associations to which belong the categories that do not have the right to a trade union, such as the civil servants, with a totalitarian organization of 230 thousand members, the railway-men, with 130 thousand members. But of all these organizations, the most interesting one, in relation to the internal problems of the fascist dictatorship, is surely that of the Fascist University Groups.

Unlike the other organizations, in the Fascist University Groups there are individuals who tend to be intellectually active. They tend to examine the problems of the Fascist dictatorship, to discuss them. These problems are not discussed in other places. There is no discussion of these problems among Fascist hierarchs; there is, instead, among the university students. Fascism has had to make a concession to them: the *Littoriali della cultura*[3]. This is one of the regime's most interesting finds. Read the newspaper accounts of them; they're very instructive. To be sure, these accounts are written or revised by tried and true journalists, but you can still see how a number of problems arise. The students discuss the character of class collaboration, the character this collaboration assumes in the current moment, if it's true the workers have the same rights as the bosses, etc. You can see all the problems that can endanger the bases of the dictatorship come to the surface. Often the problem arises of whether or not capitalism can be transcended. The nature of the Italian economy is discussed. True, discussion is carried on in fascist terms; but you can see that groups are beginning to go beyond the limits permitted by fascism and are moving toward a critique that tends to dissolve fascism's ideological edifice.

This is a very interesting problem from the standpoint of our work. As among the Young Fascists, here, too, we have the possibility of engaging in a particular form of work that starts out on the terrain of ideological debate and tends to disintegrate the ideology imposed on these individuals.

Now let's examine a question which is the point of departure of our whole policy inside the fascist organizations.

We have already referred to the crises in fascism, to their features, to the possibilities of work they offer. It must be noted that when the Fascist Party was not yet totalitarian, these crises had particular features. Underlying them was the resistance, the struggle of the petty- and middle-bourgeois cadres against the brutally capitalistic policy that the Fascist Party initiated upon taking power. It mustn't be thought that these elements were protesting in the interest of the masses. Forni, Padovani,[4] etc. were expressing the discontent of strata of the petty and middle bourgeoisie, the groups that aspired to command, to lead. This struggle turned them against the organization; it brought them into a clash with the organization of the state. However, in some places—Naples, for instance—they spoke for the masses owing to the particular conditions in these localities, where the proletariat does not dominate, where there are vast strata of petty and middle bourgeoisie, and where there are lumpen proletarians who can be mobilized to exalt a leader but not on political platforms. This feature was also found at times in other localities: Giampaolism[5] in Milan, for example. Giampaoli's rebel movement was based on semi-criminals, lumpen proletarians, old *squadristi* who were in the ranks of the Militia and wanted a return to the old-style action squads to serve their own personal interests. But there is also a large industrial proletariat in Milan. For this, Giampaoli also raised problems which interested the workers: for example, worker representation at the factory level. This rebel movement, which at the outset had the same features as the one in Naples, took on a different character in contact with the big industrial city. Giampaoli's rebel movement had a clear trade-union character.

The nature of this rebelliousness, of these crises inside the Fascist Party, changed when the Fascist Party assumed the character of the sole, totalitarian party, endeavoring to organize the masses and creating para-fascist, military, paramilitary, propaganda and trade-union organizations.

The episodes which give rise to crises now tend to have different characteristics. Since 1930, there has been a whole series of rebellions, of limited local episodes, on the part of elements tied to the working class. Militiamen have taken part in strikes, Fascists have staged open demonstrations against the bosses, led demonstrations in the factories. The protests against the bosses in 1930 in Milan were begun by Fascists.

This is the prevalent element, one that is of great importance for us; and it is an element which you will find even stronger in the Militia than in the party (although the Militia is not as large numerically, it is larger in importance) and especially in the Young Fascists. The number of protests and rebellions in the Young Fascists has grown constantly in the past years. This is a direct consequence of the nature of this organization, a nature which we have already underscored. The mass is mobilized more easily in its own immediate interests or rebels against oppression by the apparatus, etc. These episodes of rebellion inside the youth organizations are especially important and give us a particularly vast field of action.

There is a difference between today's episodes of rebellion and dissidence and those of the past. Before, a deep analysis was necessary in order to see the nature of these crises; it was not always possible to see the petty-bourgeois element that was at work. Today, it is very easy to discern the nature of these movements.

As an example, a comparison can be made with Germany. This comparison shows very clearly the differences between the two types of dictatorships and their similarities. I always insist on not confusing these two fascisms. The fundamental element of difference is represented by the fact that German fascism had succeeded in becoming a vast mass movement even before taking power. It had been able to win power by electoral means on democratic bases—limited democracy, it's true, and made more limited by the acts of violence; but all the same it had been able to win forty percent and more of the vote. This is the first element of difference.

The second element consists in the fact that before taking

power, besides having the petty and middle bourgeoisie and the agricultural workers, German fascism had masses of the unemployed in its ranks and was able, through them, to extend its influence to certain groups of factory workers and to the great peasant masses.

This is why German fascism's crises and internal struggles immediately present other characteristics. Elements in common are the rebellions of the petty- and middle-bourgeois fascist leaders against the open dictatorship of the big bourgeoisie. But in Germany these rebellions make themselves felt more strongly. They also reflect the discontent of the factory workers, of the unemployed, of the peasants won over, organized or at least influenced by fascism, who had believed that fascism would solve a whole series of problems, particularly the problem of the [economic] crisis, and now see that fascism is unable to solve any problem.

This phenomenon was seen in Italy to a more limited extent. The discontent of the workers and peasants surfaced in the Fascist organizations only later, only recently. And this is because the masses, in the past, were lined up within the structure of a whole series of old organizations, while today they are incorporated into a totalitarian structure by the Fascist Party and its parallel organizations.

Compare June 30[6] and the Matteotti crisis. There are elements of analogy. In both cases, certain adversaries—Matteotti and some fascist leaders—were killed. There were oscillations of the petty-bourgeois strata organized by fascism: in the Matteotti period, the Militia didn't respond to mobilization orders; on June 30, the Brown Shirts demonstrated deep discontent, had to be disbanded and reorganized.

In Italy, there were other parties, and the discontent of the masses was expressed through the wavering of other parties, the Aventine parties.[7] There has been some of this in Germany too, but it hasn't been the chief characteristic. The chief characteristic in Germany has been the crisis of the fascist party. There has been a decomposition of the Brown Shirts, of the factory organizations, of the protective squads. Here, too, the crisis has tended to take the same course. There has been an attempt to reorganize social democracy, the Catholics, etc. There has been a phenomenon similar to the one in Italy during the Matteotti period; but it is still in embryonic form in Germany, while in Italy it was a principal phenomenon. In Germany, the mass is already in the fascist organizations; in Italy, it was in large part outside of the old organizations, but it had not yet been incorporated into the new ones.

In Italy, as we gradually move away from fascism's seizure of power and we approach the current period, you can see that the discontent of the masses has tended to accentuate the internecine struggles in the fascist organizations. There are more and more cases of rebelliousness, which do not appear as they did before, but take the form of the struggle of the masses under certain slogans against the fascist organizations and for demands of an immediate nature.

Let's look at the latest case, the Arpinati affair.[8] This dissident movement is already at a higher level than earlier ones. No one—neither Sala nor Giampaoli—had gone so far as to formulate government programs different from those of the Fascist Party; the dissident movement kept itself inside the provincial party organizations. But Arpinati proposes a different plan for organizing the dictatorship. This is a step forward, a step forward that is a consequence of the transformations which have taken place inside the fascist organizations. Today, these leaders are in contact with the masses, whereas the old squads in 1924 and 1925 were not. These crises express something deeper today. Arpinati expresses the discontent of the petty and middle agrarian bourgeoisie of Emilia that had constituted the base of fascism in Italy; a petty and middle bourgeoisie that is discontent because it is being impoverished by high rents, by the ruin of small landholding, by the decline in the prices of farm products, by competition from big farming, etc.

lecture **5**

Fascist Trade Unions

IN THIS lesson and the next one, we shall concern ourselves with a more detailed study of the most characteristic mass organizations: the fascist trade unions and the Dopolavoro.[1] I shall speak of the fascist unions even if you have already done so in the trade -union course, because it is impossible to give a course on fascism without speaking about the unions. However, since you already have studied this subject, we shall examine it in depth from a political point of view. This will serve to refresh your knowledge and to teach you to pose the problem from the political and developmental viewpoint, to comprehend how the fascist unions have arrived at their actual form through different stages of development.

The fascist unions are fascism's principal mass organization, but they have not always been. Fascism always has had a tendency to create trade-union organizations, but this tendency has not always asserted itself in the same way. Why is there this tendency in fascism to create trade-union organizations? Fascism has posed itself the problem of directly influencing strata of workers—factory workers, farm laborers, etc.,—and of tying them to itself in an organizational form. Hence, the trade-union problem is always a current one for the Fascist Party.

This tendency is one of fascism's specific characteristics. You will also find this tendency among the prewar French nationalists, but they posed the problem differently. Only Italian fascism (and the other fascisms) presents the problem of creating a national trade-union organization as a necessary instrument in the hands of reaction.

In speaking of this, we must bear in mind who fascism's cadres are and see how they come in large part from syndicalism. They are elements who broke with the Confederation of Labor at the time of the syndicalist split, and then broke away from syndicalism at the time of the interventionist split.[2] These men had a rather profound knowledge of mass movements; they knew how these movements should be organized. By elaborating a number of theories, they arrived at the particular conception of national syndicalism, a conception which lies at the root of the ideology of the fascist unions.

What are the origins of this conception? It contained in embryonic form all the elements that later developed in fascist ideology. Originally, it still contained some residues of self-styled Marxist ideologies. It reflected backhanded attempts to join the idea of the nation to the class concept. Then it spoke of the nation standing above the classes, etc.

These paths were opened up to the theoreticians of national syndicalism not only by the reactionary bourgeois themselves, but also by men who were active and in part are still active in the ranks of the workers' movement.

They were the ones who put forth ideas about Italy as a poor nation: proletarian Italy against the capitalist nations. These ideas were being put forth by elements who had been members of the Socialist party and had became syndicalists: Enrico Ferri, Labriola, etc.[3] On this basis, there was a split in the syndicalist movement when the war broke out. The cadres who broke away were the ones who raised the trade-union problem in the Fascist Party and are still the heads of the fascist unions today.

We must never forget that Rossoni[4] was an organizer of farm workers and that at certain moments he played a very big role in the Po Valley. Let's not forget that Razza[5] also was an organizer of farm workers, in Apulia. Let's not forget that Mussolini was one of the heads of the Socialist Party. Their past enables them to have a better idea than government leaders of the past of how to intervene in order to control the masses.

Fascism raised the trade-union problem right from the outset, but it has not always followed the same method. It has arrived at the solution—the fascist trade-union monopoly—through a whole series of attempts, of experiments. It is the struggle of the masses that puts the different experiments of fascist trade-unionism to the acid test. It makes it look for different solutions; it forces it to modify the way in which the trade-union problem is framed.

The terrain of the fascist unions is the most mobile terrain in the structure of the fascist dictatorship and of fascism; the most mobile because here class relations are reflected directly and immediately.

This is proof of the exactness of the Leninist affirmation that any mass organization of workers, even the most reactionary one, inevitably becomes a theatre of class struggle, a spring-board for the class struggle.

This is our point of departure in setting our tactics for working inside the fascist unions.

It is interesting to see the different stages in the development of the trade-union movement in Italy. Your notebook does give figures, but they are somewhat confused. Still, it is interesting to make a comparison between the forces of the General Confederation of Labor on the one hand, and the fascist unions on the other, in the various moments of development of the Italian situation. It's interesting to compare the prewar figures to those for the immediate postwar period, up to 1921 and 1922; and then to the figures for 1923 and 1924, that is to say to the figures that immediately follow fascism's rise to power.

What do these figures tell us?

First of all, they tell us how the CGdL,[6] which had had 600,000 members before the war, passed the million mark in 1919 and reached 3,600,000 in 1920, a figure that also remained valid in 1921. We see a leap, a jump, from the prewar to the postwar figures, and then we see an even larger leap from 1919 to 1920-21. This is a translation in terms of trade-union membership of the modifications in the Italian situation. The drive of the masses in Italian society made itself felt formidably; and for Italian society, which was unable to resist it, this drive meant that the majority of the workers and laborers were joining the class unions and *waging disciplined struggle*. This imposing class force appeared on the scene of Italian society and, in spite of the reformist leaders, struggled day in, day out.

This modification in social relations had to lead to a modification of political relations: either the admittance of the masses into the state structure or the dictatorship of the proletariat. Italian capitalism could have accepted the admittance of the masses into the state structure. Indeed, fascism has used this as a foothold. Fascism destroyed the class organizations, but then set about rebuilding the working-class organizations and bringing them into the structure of the fascist dictatorship. From the general theoretical viewpoint, the question is raised as follows: let's keep the masses organized, but let's imbue their organizations with a reactionary character.

Giolitti proposed to reach the selfsame objective by a different route. The path he followed was that of corrupting the reformist leaders. But Giolitti's policy was destined to fail since the pressure of the masses was too strong.

The other path which inevitably presented itself was that of the struggle for power. When the working class has organized itself, when it has acquired great maturity and its organizations a great breadth, then it is impossible to continue without posing the problem of power. But when the problem of power is posed, the bourgeoisie intervenes. So the third path presents itself: the path of fascist dictatorship.

The figures clearly indicate that there were only two ways out: either proletarian dictatorship or fascist dictatorship. Let's examine these figures.

Of the 2,180,000 members of the CGdL as of December 31, 1920, we can see a compact mass of 760,000 farm workers. Then came the great organizations of the construction workers, the metalworkers, the textile workers, etc., each with a membership of between 140,000 and 180,000. We see that the great mass was represented by the farm workers. This was the social structure of the General Confederation of Labor, a structure that had a decisive weight in subsequent modifications.

Later, immediately after fascism took power, the Confederation's official year-end statistics for 1923 gave a total of 212,000 members. If we make an analysis of these 212,000 members, we are struck by one thing: the 760,000 farm workers had been reduced to 20,000. This impressive force had almost completely disappeared.

And now let's give the figures for the fascist unions. Before fascism took power, its trade-union organizations had 558,000 members, half of whom—276,000—came from agriculture. The fascist unions counted 1,764,000 members in 1924; of these, 694,000 were farm workers. These figures are all subject to criticism; it can be demonstrated how they are not true. But a fundamental fact remains, and it is the shift of many organized workers into the camp of the fascist unions. This was the main blow fascism dealt against the General Confederation of Labor in the countryside, against the agricultural laborers' organizations. It was in this field that fascism was first able to boast of success. This boasting had a basis in reality. The figures were not given at random; they truly reflected a class shift in the countryside, a shift of certain rural masses towards the fascist trade-union structure. To better understand this fact, bear in mind that fascism also counts sharecroppers, tenant farmers, etc., in its trade unions.

We now have come up to 1924; we are in the first period of the fascist dictatorship. How was the trade-union problem posed at this time?

At first sight—outwardly, we say—the trade-union problem was put on the grounds of competition with the other unions. At first, up to the moment fascism took power, this movement had gone nowhere. There had been something here and there, but this had not solved the problem of conquering the mass. This conquest began only after the seizure of power, when, while the competitive aspect was outwardly maintained, the pressure of the state apparatus intervened in fact. An extremely interesting phenomenon in this period was the statistical shift in favor of the fascist unions in every category. Part of the mass stayed in the Catholic organizations, but these don't concern us today.

But who directed the strikes in this period? Who controlled most of the shop committees? The CGdL.

What did this mean? It meant that the nucleus of the most advanced workers, the backbone of the organization, remained in the class unions. And the mass, even that part of it which had gone over to the fascist unions, continued to be led by the CGdL. Ten thousand metalworkers remained in the FIOM,[7] for example. But these 10,000 formed a nucleus which had a large influence over all the other metalworkers, who, even if they no longer carried a CGdL membership card, still followed its directives.

Let's look at the FIAT metalworkers' strike of 1925. The initiative was taken by the fascist unions. They had been able to bring several thousand workers into their ranks on competitive grounds, and now, still on these grounds, they tried to win over the mass with wage demands and demands for an increase in the piece-work rates. This attempt was frustrated at once. Why? Because the trade-union steering nucleus, which was Communist in Turin, correctly raised the problem: So you're talking like this? So you want to strike? Fine, then we'll strike. The strike was called and passed into the hands of the FIOM. This is an example of exploiting the legal possibilities, the study of which is very interesting. It demonstrates that fascist trade-unionism cannot develop on competitive grounds.

The same thing happened in the elections of the shop committees in all the factories of Italy. I don't recall a single case in which the fascist unions won a majority. They were always beaten, gathering a minimal percentage of the votes. Only in one or two cases did they obtain high percentages; for example, when they formed a coalition with the reformists at the FIAT Lingotto works at the end of 1925. There, the Communists were already going it alone and had lost city-wide leadership of the FIOM in 1923.

Another decisive fact to bear in mind in order to comprehend the growth of the fascist unions is the influence they were able to cast over the mass through the weight of the state structure. We mustn't forget this. But we also mustn't forget the great resistance the workers put up before joining the fascist unions. This indicates that we have a ripe terrain for our work in these unions.

The fascist unions must not be regarded as a bloc without conflicts, without contradictions. The fascist unions represent a terrain on which we can see continual struggles unfold, on which we can see a constant modification of the class relations and of the forms of organization.

Fascism was unable to solve the problem on competitive grounds. It couldn't succeed even with the help of the reformists. Fascism saw that despite the fact it had its own organization, it wasn't able to dominate the class organizations. As soon as a conflict would arise, the fascist unions would be pushed aside and the struggle would continue under the leadership of the Communists. Attempts were made to give new vitality to the fascist unions through an accord with the leadership of the CGdL. This explains the transformations which took place in the organization of the CGdL from 1923 to '26. The CGdL of '26 was not the CGdL of '22. It was completely different from the organizational standpoint. It had been fascistized. It no longer was the same organization that had held the Verona Convention where, in spite of everything, we had been able to win a minority of 800,000 votes. This no longer was possible in 1923 at the Confederation's Milan Convention. The CGdL's structure had changed. In 1924, the whole organization was bureaucratized and organized from above. This took place at the time the bourgeoisie was creating its reactionary unions. The CGdL's reformist heads followed the same process as the bourgeoisie and repeatedly offered the bourgeoisie their services. But fascism was unable to solve the problem even on this terrain.

Notwithstanding the transformation of the General Confederation of Labor, despite the tricks it devised, the mass of its membership, whose nucleus we have discussed, fell more and more under the Communists' influence. This was the decisive moment. The exceptional laws arrived on the scene when the leaders were already completely fascistized and the rebellion of the masses was bringing them over to the Communists.

February 20[8] therefore has an enormous importance for us. *It marked the break of the masses with the line followed by the reformist heads. Because of this, February 20 has an extremely important political and historical value.*

Given the impossibility of solving the problem on competitive grounds, even with the help of the reformists, the fascist unions were left with only one way out: to go over to the terrain of totalitarianism. And so we have the series of fascist labor laws: the Vidoni Palace Pact, the Law of April 3, 1926, the Charter of Labor, etc.[9] These laws established the fascist unions' monopoly.

The fascist unions became the only legal class organization, the only organization allowed to conclude labor contracts. There was still the right to form de facto unions, which, however, could not conclude labor contracts. This right could not be made effective.

Our notes say that there was only one case of the creation of a de facto union. It must be recalled in this regard that the Catholics maintained union-style organizations called study groups[10] inside the sphere of Catholic Action until two years ago. These organizations remained standing until the last conflict between the Church and fascism.

When fascism established totalitarianism in the trade-union field, the problem was settled. But it would reappear in new forms. We thus can see a typical change of front.

Initially, all of fascism's efforts had been directed at destroying the mass organizations of a class character. After 1926, its efforts were directed at creating fascist mass organizations. This change was more visible in the unions than elsewhere. The statistics reflect the dying-off of the old class trade-union organizations and the growth of the fascist organizations.

I will not dwell on the details of the Vidoni Palace Pact and the 1926 trade-union law. You will find what you need in the material.

It must be said that the trade-union structure after the Law of 1926 was not uniform. The first observation to make is the big difference that existed from category to category. The fascist union was a different thing from one category to another. This was connected to the fact that in some categories fascism had succeeded in creating its own unions by merging with the old class unions and completely appropriating the apparatus of the pre-existing Confederation. In other categories, instead, the class organization had been completely destroyed and the fascist union created *ex novo*.

The printers offer us an example of the first kind. In the printers' field, the fascists were unable to break down the organizations affiliated with the Confederation. The Confederation-affiliated organization kept its cadres and membership intact for a long time. The origins of the resistance of the printers' organization must be sought in its guild-like nature. What happened? The organization passed over to fascism bag and baggage. It can be said that there was not a single printer who did not join the fascist trade-union organization. Our attempts to build a class organization of printers after they had crossed over to the fascist camp did not succeed. This organization went over to the fascist unions completely because the printers' organizational forms permitted this crossover. The same happened for the glassmakers, the hatters and several other guild-like categories.

But when we come to the metalworkers, the chemical workers, the textile workers—in a word, to those categories that had a class-based organization—then there was the problem of destroying their organizations and creating new ones.

You cannot find large modifications in the fascist organizations of printers at the rank-and-file level. The same forms of organization were preserved. The same office was retained. The system of collectors, of division into categories and subcategories, of union control over moves from one category to the next, etc.—all this was preserved. Not even the structure of the labor contract was changed. The same can't be said of the other organizations.

A second observation regards the modifications which the fascist unions have undergone in the course of their development since 1926. The fascist unions have changed form four or five times. Their present form is the result of a whole series of attempts and struggles. In 1927, the fascist union leaders wanted to create a workers' organization similar to the General Confederation of Labor. The structure was to have been based on the craft federations, which then would have been unified in a confederation, the Confederation of Fascist Trade Unions. It was at this time that we committed our biggest mistake in the field of our work in the fascist unions.

For the very fact that they had the same structure as the Confederation of Labor, these organizations presented possibilities of work which would not reappear. Only now, in part, are they beginning to present themselves again. In 1927-28, the fascist unions were in crisis without our having done any work. The signs of this crisis were visible in the discussion on the shop stewards, in the way the Rome Congress of fascist unions was held in 1928, etc.

Concerning the problem of the shop stewards, we can see how the fascist unions not only wanted to continue to use the organizational forms of the General Confederation of Labor, but were also demanding the same rights as it. They wanted to have representation inside the factory. The Vidoni Palace Pact prohibited this instead. No organization is allowed inside the factory, said the pact. It therefore raised the problem of destroying the shop committees. Hence, the fascist union leaders were demanding a revision of the Vidoni Palace Pact. Mussolini's arbitration intervened and was favorable to the bosses. Mussolini said: there must be only one power inside the factory.

The Rome Congress also presents several considerably interesting facets. The Fascist officials, whom we had never worked on, spoke in this congress just as we are telling our comrades to speak out today in the fascist unions. They made a harsh critique of the measures the bosses were taking.

The structure of the fascist unions had to be transformed to make of them an instrument of control. The very numerous transformations began at this time. These transformations have always involved the problem of the functioning of the local unions.

At first, the trade unions were based on the local organizations. Then, these were set aside and the congresses were held on a provincial basis. Thus, with continual oscillations, we come up to 1932. The fascist trade-union apparatus tended to break the discipline of the fascist organizational scheme and give birth to local unions. There was a tendency in the fascist unions always to demand and, in fact, to win union representation inside the factories. Fascist union representation at the factory level tended to spread and appeared almost everywhere. *The local unions and the shop stewards were the hottest terrain for the fascist unions.*

In 1932 and 1933, a strong blow was dealt to the local organizations and shop stewards—this through the Law of January 1933, which was the result of a series of measures taken in '32 to suppress the mass movements that were tending to grow inside of the fascist unions.

Some say this was the end of fascist trade-unionism. This is not true, or rather it is true only if the statement is taken literally. Since the law, the fascist unions still exist, the problems still exist. An expression of this is to be had in the Law of September 1934.

This law recognized the local unions and gave them the function of concluding labor contracts in the first instance. The whole fascist trade-union organization was made over on the basis of the election of lower-level officials. Before, these officials were designated from above. Now, the leaders —essentially, the shop stewards, secretary and steering committeemen of the local unions—are elected by membership meetings.

This is the point which interests us most. Why did these transformations take place in 1934? The explanation must be this: fascism is now busy with the job of organizing the corporative state, and the trade-union law of 1934 is one of the elements of its organization. The law was made for the purpose of giving the impression that the corporative state is being organized on a democratic or quasi-democratic basis; and this just when every form of bourgeois democracy is being set aside, when there is talk of eliminating Parliament, when the second plebiscite[11] has been held. Fascism is modifying the trade-union structure in a maneuver to draw nearer to the masses.

In your studies you must make a comparative analysis of the most important laws. The Law of 1933 was still a law of struggle, but of struggle against the workers' attempts to express their interests from within the fascist unions themselves. The law represented the maximum bureaucratization of the unions. In '34 we have another zigzag, another attempt to use more "democratic" forms in order to establish a closer contact between the masses and the unions.

What are the weakest points in the fascist unions, the points on which we must concentrate our work?

Essentially, there are three: 1) the factory and union representation at the factory level; 2) the local union and the membership meeting; 3) the conclusion of the labor contract.

Fascism is constantly discussing these points, constantly changing its organizational forms. It is here that we must concentrate our work.

It must be remembered that even after the latest measures,

the fascist union is never uniform throughout Italy. In their reports, our rank-and-file comrades and our regional leaders indicate that notable region-to-region differences exist. No matter how many examples we make, we still see that there always are some local differences. This is important in determining our position.

Union meetings, for example: should we attend them or not? Before, the Party gave orders to boycott them. In some cities, the fascist unions had to force the workers to stay for meetings. Today, we say we must go to them. Today, the Fascists no longer force attendance at meetings; there's a tendency to go to them on one's own. But the Party material we receive from the South and also from some localities in the North shows that the problem is still framed in these places in the same way as in 1927. You will find a mass that still refuses to go to meetings and takes an abstentionist stance.

In one meeting, for example, a speaker pauses for a few moments to catch his breath and the workers leave, pretending they think the speech is over. This is a demonstration, but a demonstration of passive resistance. There is no struggle to it. In Naples, for instance, union meetings are called to which propagandists, members of the Fascist University Groups, come to make speeches. These meetings are not called in order to discuss questions of work. What must we do? We must turn these meetings into meetings where union problems are discussed. The comrades, instead, have taken an attitude of sabotage. They organize out-of-place applause to upset the speakers, use every method to obstruct the smooth progress of the meetings, etc. In Apulia, union meetings never are called; indeed, measures are taken to keep the workers from entering union headquarters more than one-at-a-time. Here, a new problem is raised. What must we do? I think we must demand that the fascist union hold meetings. We must say to the fascist union official: tell us a little about how you have defended our interests! We must proceed from this point.

But there are different forms not only in different localities, but even in the same locality. In La Spezia, for example, fascist union meetings were banned after the demonstrations of the past year. From that moment on, the comrades didn't know how to proceed and brought their action to a halt. What should we have done? We ourselves ought to have called meetings through specially prepared elements.

The adaptation of our work to the fascist unions' forms of organization and of life is one of the most difficult things. There are many mistakes and failings in this field.

The conclusion of labor contracts represents another weak-point. Who ought to conclude them? According to the law, the local union. But as far as we know, it doesn't. There's a tendency to conclude contracts on a regional scale and then to bring them to the Council of Corporations for ratification. Here is more ground for our work. Here, too, the terrain varies. When the labor contract is made on the regional scale, we must say: we want the contract to be made on the local level. Here we are acting on the grounds of fascist law, but we are starting out from these grounds in order to sharpen the conflicts inside the fascist organizations and mobilize the masses.

But the main axis of our work in the fascist union organizations is represented by the fascist shop stewards. We must demand that there be a shop steward and that he be elected.

There are clauses in labor contracts which it is interesting to know. The FIAT contract, for example, permits workers' committees for checking on the application of piece-work rates. Our comrades have never noticed it, and yet this is a very important problem.

On this terrain, we must start out, when necessary, even from the most backward forms, pressuring, when it is the case, for the naming of a union dues collector. Then, through the dues collector, by enlarging his functions, we must try to create a shop steward.

Every time we raise this question, the problem shifts, is raised more acutely, and fascism is forced to annul its previous orders.

In our work of exploiting the legal possibilities inside the fascist unions, we must always remember how this organization represents a body of class relations; and how it has been conceived in different ways by fascism in the various periods of fascism's development, and even in the same period, depending on the different situations which fascism has had to handle in various places.

But we will talk more about this in the discussion period.

lecture 6

The "Dopolavoro"[1]

WE HAVE made an examination in which we have underscored the differences which exist among fascism's various mass organizations; and we have seen how, on the basis of these differences, we determine our tactics, our stance and the forms to adopt in our work in these organizations—work to be carried out from the inside and the outside. First we looked at the political organization, the party, which has a tendency to become a mass organization. Then we spoke of the military and propaganda organizations, characteristic of which are the Young Fascists, and we dwelt on the trade-union organizations, coercive mass organizations whose mass character is therefore not broader than that of the foregoing ones.

Today we come to the broadest of the fascist organizations. I say organizations in the narrow sense of the word and I raise this reservation because there are other organizations: winter relief is an organization and embraces a much larger mass than all the other fascist organizations, but it doesn't have membership cards, headquarters or membership dues.

The Dopolavoro has not always been the numerically largest organization of fascism, but it has been the broadest in its purposes, in its origins, in its organizational forms. Fascism boasts of having invented the Dopolavoro back at the time of the first *fasci di combattimento*. This is not true. It's true these may have offered sports and cultural activities, etc., but this was not yet the Dopolavoro. Only later, only on the eve of the promulgation of the exceptional laws, in 1926, was fascism presented with the problem of creating a real mass organization.

It can be said—it's good to insist on the dates so that you can familiarize yourselves with them and get an idea of the development of fascism—that this organization was created at the beginning of 1926. If you remember what we have said on the development of fascism, you will easily understand how this was one of the measures for arriving at the establishment of the corporative state. The Dopolavoro institution is one of the organizations of the corporative state.

When the Dopolavoro arose, it was not faced with the problem of competition. It set itself up in terms similar to other [fascist] organizations. Meanwhile, by 1926, the trade unions, too, no longer were acting on competitive grounds; they had a monopoly and thus had no problem of competition. There were other reasons as well: *a centralized class organization for satisfying the educational, cultural and sports needs of the masses did not exist and had never existed in Italy.* This was one of the most serious failings of the Italian workers' movement, particularly the postwar movement. Some attempts had been made, but they always had a purely local character (in Turin, for example). There were also associations linked to pre-existing organizational forms. For example, there was a wide network of cultural associations, clubs, etc., in Venezia Giulia; but this was a legacy left to Italy by Austrian social democracy when Italy annexed Venezia Giulia.

What forms of organization existed in this field? Characteristic of them everywhere was their very simple scope, which didn't go beyond providing an evening's entertainment, a place to drink a glass of wine, and things of this type. Most of the organizations of the time have to be seen from this standpoint. In Emilia, there were a great many wine clubs pursuing these purposes. These clubs also existed in Piedmont and, generally speaking, in all the wine-making regions. The masses created this type of organization as a mean of fighting the wine crisis. Typical in this regard is the fact that in Novara the members of these clubs had to drink a certain amount of wine each week.

These forms did not exist in the South, or at least they existed to a very limited extent—this because the forms of organization of the working people of the South were very limited.

Sports associations had been growing a little before the war and immediately after it. The Socialist Party made some attempts to create its own organizations of this kind, but it achieved few results due, among other things, to the strong anti-sports prejudices that subsisted in the party.

Only in the final years, in 1922, '23, '24 and '25, when the real class organizations had been or were on the way to being destroyed, when the trade-union councils, class unions, cooperatives, etc. had been disbanded or destroyed, could one note a tendency to create workers' sports associations on a neighborhood basis, at times on a city-wide basis, sometimes even on a factory basis.

What we are saying doesn't mean that workers' sports associations had not existed before. For example, in Turin we had a big moutaineering society. There were many small associations in Milan and many more in Lombardy. But these had a limited local character. There never was a national organization in Italy; there never was a congress of the existing organizations.

The masses were drawn away from the clubs, cooperatives, etc., and tended to join these organizations. The industrialists supported this trend and facilitated the creation of factory sports groups. Many factory sports associations, devoted especially to football, were founded. They enjoyed some success. For example, the FIAT workers' sports society grew reasonably well, but with the participation of the bosses. Many recreation associations were formed at the factory level at the bosses' initiative *in order to divert the workers from the class struggle.*

I have mentioned this subject because it is fundamental in determining our tactics. The fascist dictatorship has organized the Dopolavoro and has forced the masses to join it, giving the masses a certain amount of benefits, satisfying to some degree a need of the Italian working masses.

Don't be alarmed by this statement: the Dopolavoro does satisfy some of the Italian workers' needs. I will explain what I mean to say.

Bear in mind that the only club that could be found before in the cities, villages and rural areas of the South was the gentlemen's club. Today there is a local Dopolavoro in almost every town. These organizations can be defined as compulsory, but the worker does find in them a place where he can pass the evening, where he can stay warm when the weather is cold, where he can play cards, where he can drink a glass of wine if he has the money, etc. These organizations are very important as mass organizations, for they represent a link fascism has forged to tie the masses to itself.

How has fascism managed to create this organization, one of the broadest fascist organizations, which counts two million members and which branches out into thousands of local chapters that are different in nature and distinguish themselves for a higher level of activity than the Fascist Party and even the fascist unions? How has such an organization been created?

Fascism in part has created new organizations, in part has brought into action all the means at its disposal to absorb the different forms of recreational and cultural organizations which the masses had shaped for themselves before the foundation of the Dopolavoro, and to absorb all the new organizations which were being formed in that period. *For this, the Dopolavoro is one of the most complex organizations of the fascist dictatorship.* The Dopolavoro is not a monolithic organization like the Fascist Party, not a structurally homogenous organization like the Young Fascists; not cut from one mold like the fascist trade unions.

It is a complex organization. Not only does it have different branches, but at the base it has different types of chapters depending on the ends which the organization is pursuing, or depending on the masses with which it is in contact, and also depending on the forms of organization which have existed in a given locality on a particular ground.

Let's look at the first differentiation, the one among the various branches and various activities. In this field, you will find organizations whose mass character is very limited. For example, certain sports associations affiliated with the Dopolavoro have a professional character. In general, all the sports associations that are clubs—Juventus, for example—which you have to be either a professional or wealthy to join, belong to this category. These are not mass organizations. Their entire activity consists in choosing some of the best athletes in their localities and turning them into professionals. Also of this kind are societies concerned with the arts in the narrowest sense of the word—*il Carro di Tespi*,[2] for instance. Fascism has also tried to create a mass theatre, but has not succeeded. Last year, an attempt was made in Florence to act out an episode from the March on Rome, etc. This attempt was a complete fiasco, as could be seen by reading between the lines of the fascist newspapers themselves. Little by little, the masses grew tired and went away. There is a contradiction between mass theatre and the ideological basis of fascism. These attempts hit it off big when aimed in the patriotic, nationalist direction. Here it is easier to find individuals who, influenced by nationalist sentiments, might be receptive to these exercises. But not much is being done in this field. The most popular figures of the Italian Risorgimento—Garibaldi, for instance—are left out. They are troublesome to fascism; they are inconvenient. These organizations therefore address themselves to a culturally more elevated stratum.

The bulk of Dopolavoro organizations have a different character, a real mass character. They are in direct contact with the mass of workers, satisfy certain needs of the workers, comprise a large number of associations created by the workers themselves and incorporated into the Dopolavoro by fascism.

We have said that besides the division by branch of activity, there is also one by type of association. Here, too, we have a number of types. For our purposes, there are two fundamental ones: *the old workers' clubs absorbed by the Dopolavoro and the Dopolavoro clubs founded as such.* We can draw yet another distinction by type: the factory-level and territorial Dopolavoros.

What are the numerical relations among the various types? It is impossible to obtain figures regarding the distinction between old and new associations; fascism is very careful not to draw this distinction. But we can get an idea of how they compare from the data supplied us by our regional leaders and rank-and-file organizations. It appears that the old clubs predominate in rural areas, the new ones in the cities; the old clubs prevalently in zones where there was a network of working-class cultural organizations which at a certain point stopped resisting and joined the Dopolavoro system. In the province of Novara, for example, where there was a wide network of clubs, the officers of these clubs preferred at a given moment to allow them to be fascistized in order to keep the organizations from being destroyed and to retain the funds which they had accumulated. The members at first put up resistance, then they resigned themselves. The advance of fascism was resisted up to the very end in Turin. The Fascists destroyed the trade unions and cooperatives, expunged the neighborhood clubs one by one. The neighborhood clubs had a conspicuously political character since the old Socialist members had fought to give them this nature. Unlike Novara, where most clubs are of the old type, most organizations in Turin have been created from the ground up. Even in Turin, however, there are some old organizations, and they are the same ones we neglected almost totally during the Red Years. There are family clubs, neighborhood clubs, sports clubs, etc., which stayed independent for a long time. One organization of this type is Turin Family, which the comrades joined very late and which now retains its old structure as part of the Dopolavoro system.

You will not find the old neighborhood clubs in the Dopolavoros in Turin; you will in Novara, and you will also find them in Emilia, in Venetia and in Lombardy, even on the outskirts of Milan.

Let's examine another point: the difference between company and territorial organizations. In 1933 only 3,000 out of 18,000 local Dopolavoros were set up on the company level. They were therefore an absolute minority. This shows the Dopolavoro's character well. If you look at statistics on the Dopolavoro's membership, you will see that its social composition is characteristic. In 1930, when the Dopolavoro had not yet arrived at the 2,000,000 members it has today but counted between 1,300,000 and 1,400,000 members, there were 600,000 industrial workers, 260,000 peasants, etc. If you take the social composition, you will see how industrial workers were preponderant, accounting for roughly half of the total organized forces, and exceeding half if we add the railwaymen and other transport workers whom the statistics list under other figures.

If you take the 1933 figure for factory-level chapters, you will find that only a part of the 2,000,000 total members were in the 3,000 company chapters. This means that the whole mass of workers is not in the company-level organizations, but is also to be found in the territorial ones. The Dopolavoro system is highly ramified. What, in fact, is a local Dopolavoro? Workers whose companies have a Dopolavoro often prefer to go to a neighborhood one instead; there they can find the particular forms of activity to which they want to devote themselves.

There is also a structural difference among the various types of organizations. The difference is evident between the old and new clubs. What happens when an old club joins the Dopolavoro system? The officers hold discussions, talk over what should be done, etc. These discussions involve the acceptance of control by supervisors. As a rule, once the supervisor has entered the organization, the democratic forms should be suppressed. But this happens only for a short while. After a while, the old statute is revived in most cases. After several years, the new ties tend to slacken, the old habits are resumed.

But this happens only for a short while. After a while, the old statute is revived in most cases. After several years, the new ties tend to slacken, the old habits are resumed.

In the new clubs, instead, the organization is typically fascist. The mass belonging to them and influenced by them has been forced to join by means of violence or indirect constraint. There is absolutely no form of democratic organization. Here, merely raising the problem of the election of officers can make this mass break up. But under pressure from the mass, even these clubs tend to take a more democratic character, to move toward the election of officers; and elements come to the fore in them who enjoy the confidence of the mass or try to take over the official posts.

This tendency does exist. On the basis of this tendency, and taking into account the fact that these organizations satisfy certain needs of the members, we determine our tactics.

The company-level clubs are even less democratic, more tightly controlled; it is harder to work in them. I do not recall a single case of work being done in a company Dopolavoro. This is related to another fact: membership in the company Dopolavoro is mandatory in most cases since the membership dues are withheld from the pay envelope. Thus, in theory, all of a company's employees are members of its Dopolavoro if one exists. There are exceptions, however. But who frequents this Dopolavoro? Not all the workers. The old workers don't frequent it; only the young ones do.

In Turin, there are neighborhood clubs and company Dopolavoros. The latter are much more attractive, much better equipped, but you will not find the old worker in them. In the company Dopolavoro, you find almost exclusively the new workers, the youths to whom it offers advantages for outings, skiing, skating, etc., and so many other things of this kind to which the old workers are not accustomed and does not feel drawn. The old worker would feel here as if he were in a foreign land. He finds a more familiar milieu, instead, in the neighborhood Dopolavoro clubs. He can drink a glass of wine there. Being there doesn't arouse such repugnance in him.

Another difference between the two types consists in the fact that the active, leading elements of the company Dopolavoro are elements who already have all the characteristics of the petty bourgeois. A comrade reported that the most assiduous frequenters of the Cooperative Alliance's Dopolavoro were the clerical workers. The production workers who frequented it were few. In the FIAT Dopolavoro, most of the active elements are clerical workers.

There is a danger in this. Elements who tend to lose their proletarian character come to the fore; the attempt is made to instill a petty-bourgeois character in the workers who belong to these organizations. Some begin to think: if I get on good terms with the boss or the foreman, maybe I'll be better off. And so they drop out of the class struggle.

This is a danger, a danger we must combat. We are not combating it sufficiently, and this is a major failing.

What do the local Dopolavoros do? They carry on a whole series of activities. The benefits the workers have are manifold. They get special terms, reductions for theatre and movie tickets, discounts on food and clothing bought in certain department stores, on outings. Then they also have some form of welfare. In some cases, the Dopolavoro tends to take on mutual-aid functions and assists, for example, needy families of disabled workers, etc., etc.

It's time to stop thinking the workers shouldn't engage in sports. Even the smallest advantages are not scorned by the workers. The worker always looks for the smallest thing he can find in order to improve his lot. Just being able to sit in a room and listen to the radio in the evening is something that brings pleasure. We cannot inveigh against the worker who agrees to enter this room for the mere fact that the Fascist symbol is on the door.

We must remember that the Dopolavoro is fascism's broadest organization; that our tactics must be broader than elsewhere because, given the way the Dopolavoro is set up, we can tie up with broader strata than in other organizations.

The position of the Youth Federation and the Party with regard to the Dopolavoro has not always been what it is today. The first position the Youth Federation took was: *Out of the Dopolavoro!* This was the position in 1926 and '27. There was a discussion, and some comrades said it was not correct, but this is the line that was taken. This position was criticized by the Party and the KIM,[3] and was supplanted by a new one which represented a step forward, but which, too, was false: *Let's join the Dopolavoro in order to break it up.*

Why were these positions wrong? Because inasmuch as the masses join the Dopolavoro for the advantages it offers, we have no prospect of keeping them out of the organization. By the end of 1926, we no longer had any such prospect. And so where the masses go, we must go too. But there are other reasons as well why these postions were wrong. We were asking that the Dopolavoro be broken up. But what can we ourselves give in exchange *today* to the factory workers, to the peasants, to the office workers? Nothing. To take this postion means we are telling the workers: you must not engage in sports, you must not devote yourselves to any cultural activity but underground cultural activity, you must not have any place for recreation. These directives smack of the old position of the Socialist Party, which completely ignored these elemental needs of the masses.

We must realize that the masses do well to go there since they can tie the problem of the struggle against fascism to the problem of satisfying a number of given needs; since they can turn these organizations into centers of resistance, centers for the struggle against fascism.

Then weight must be given again to the differences among the individual local chapters. In many regions, there are workers' clubs which the members view with sympathy, organizations which cannot be called coercive.

But this consideration apart, *if we take the path of abstentionism, the path of mere disruption, we are denying ourselves a chance to do organizing among the masses of young workers, and not only of young workers but of workers in general: workers to whom a library means something, an excursion, etc. means something, and who belong to this organization. If we take this position, we are cutting ourselves off from the masses.*

Our line must be to go into the Dopolavoro without qualms and reservations. In the Dopolavoro, we must do a particular job of leading the class struggle with more advanced forms and objectives than are possible in the fascist trade unions.

Let's see how the problem of entering the Dopolavoro presents itself. We have encountered and still do encounter stiff resistance on this terrain. The comrades who put up this resistance do not realize that not only are they denying themselves the possibility of doing mass organizing, but that they find themselves in an unfavorable position from the personal standpoint, from the standpoint of persecution by the police. When he is a member of the Dopolavoro, even the comrade most known to the police has at his disposal a series of possibilities for somehow evading its control.

A symptomatic fact: the comrades who get out of prison never spontaneously frequent the Dopolavoro. We ask: when you got out of prison, did you try to approach the clubs you once belonged to? We note that nearly all of them do not frequent any of these organizations. They believe there's a moral breach in this, an insuperable abyss. They believe they shouldn't go there because these are fascist organizations. We must lay down the clearest possible line: *even the oldest, even the best-known comrades can and must join the Dopolavoro and remain in it until they are thrown out.* And the attempt to throw them out may be an element of struggle in certain cases. If they insist and say they want to remain, that they have the right to since they regularly pay their dues, etc., it is not improbable that they will move the mass in their favor and gain its sympathy. Their mistaken position also reflects the attitude of old elements, of old workers who look with horror on the Fascist emblem. This feeling of theirs is something to be respected in that they show they know what a principle is. But their position is wrong because it is not in this way that one sticks to one's principles; otherwise, we could become hermits, go into a forest and worship communism there.

Our duty is to join these organizations and organize the struggle for our principles inside of them. In the struggle, we must start from the most elementary motives, and it is precisely in these organizations that we can offer the most elementary resistance to fascism. We must enter these organizations precisely for this. Even at the Party's center, some comrades had been repeating the incorrect position. But they were defeated. We told them: instead of helping the factory workers tie up with the masses, you are clinging to the political limitation created by fascism and produced by fascism's pressure on the old working-class and Party militants.

Thus, we must get to work inside this organization. But how to work? Here is where we broaden our tactics. We do not enter this organization to break it up or to work in it separated from the great mass. For example, some comrades have proposed this formula: Join the Dopolavoro and organize separate activities; when the Dopolavoro hold demonstrations, our comrades should go somewhere else. There is only one correct element to this; namely, that the comrades must try to tie up with each other, to work as a faction, as an opposition group. But all this must be done in the midst of the mass, without ever loosing contact with the mass. Not to go to big demonstrations, even if they are organized for nationalistic purposes, is an error. If there's a nationalist demonstration—for example, a visit to the Monument to the War Dead—should the comrades go or not? It's clear they must go. Only in a few cases is it admissible for them not to go: when the comrades have such strength within the organization as to get the mass to openly approve the decision not to go. But to reach this point it is necessary to have already won the mass over. If one thousand or two thousand workers go to a demonstration, the fifty comrades must go too in order to keep in touch with the mass, speak to it, stir doubts, provoke conflicts between the organizers of the demonstration and the mass. This is our job.

The fundamental line we are following today is *the takeover of Dopolavoro organizations by the workers*. This, too, has been much-discussed; we've already mentioned this. The slogan *"The Dopolavoro to the workers"* was justly criticized since it might have produced illusion that the Dopolavoro system as such could be taken over and transformed into a class organization. That cannot happen without a break in the fascist dictatorship. But can an individual Dopolavoro organization be taken over? Yes. Are the workers tending in this direction? Yes. An elementary form can already be noted in the organizations. To begin with, the Dopolavoro center is taken over. Lately, there have even been reports of subversive songs having been sung in some Dopolavoro centers. This in itself represents the winning of some liberties. Then, the attempt is made to assume the administration. This is tried first in furtive forms: the old officer who accepts the supervisor but with the mental reservation of doing as he sees fit. This is an interesting but dangerous tendency. If we don't put ourselves at the head of this tendency and channel it, not only will it not disturb fascism, but the organization will tend to adapt itself; it will adjust to the current situation. This is why fascism doesn't always react openly against these organizations. Fascism adapts itself; and so the old officer imagines he is not adapting to fascism and then ends up by really adapting to it. This is where the danger lies: the adaptation of the workers and old officers to fascism.

The way to combat this danger is to put ourselves at the head of the tendency to oppose fascism and to give it a class content. What the mass does unconsciously, we must make it do consciously, and then we must make it push ahead. This organization must be turned into a center of activity against fascism, which can assume the most diverse forms.

It's clear we can't say: demand that Mussolini be shot. We would be committing a mistake because we would be exposing ourselves. We would get ourselves thrown out of the Dopolavoro, the mass wouldn't follow us, and everything would end there. The issues on which we act must, instead, be found inside the Dopolavoro itself. We must seize on demands proper to the Dopolavoro—demands regarding sports, culture, etc.—and on democratic issues.

We have done very little in the first field. The Youth Federation has done something in that it has raised demands that tend to have this characteristic. There is some activity in the field of sports, in the field of the struggle against chauvinism, but nothing or next to nothing in many other fields. Little, for example, in the cultural field. There are few cases of comrades who have tried to set up a library with books which have a class content. But even in the few cases in which this has been done, it has been done only halfway. There ought to have been an effort to undertake cultural work, to circulate and explain the works of Gorky, Tolstoy and others whose content could be subversive in Italy today, and to contrast the ideas contained in these books to the ideas of fascism. Conflicts can be created even on this terrain. But it's difficult. Above all, it's difficult for this form to reach the highest level, to assume the character of a national manifestation. Difficult, but not impossible.

It is necessary to request library books which talk about the USSR—there are many that are legal in Italy—and to begin a discussion of Soviet questions. A legal or semi-legal form of organization of friends of the USSR is created in this way. Characteristic is the case of a Trieste Dopolavoro that organized a trip to the USSR, went as far as Odessa, and made contact with the local organizations. On their return, all the participants were arrested. Even so, something was accomplished. And mark the fact that this happened right in Trieste, where the comrades still understand nothing about working in the enemy organizations and are among the most reluctant to do so.

Another activity consists in demanding things. For example: out with the Fascist supervisor! Control of the administration by the members. Election to offices. A good job cannot be done here especially if every minor incident isn't used as a springboard. For example: it's rumored that something has been lifted from the organization's treasury. Immediately we raise the problem of checking its content.

A very difficult terrain is that of the company Dopolavoros. Here, the demand for elections is very advanced for the members. It means shattering the whole organizational structure. This can be achieved only after much work. What should we do? We should bring two hundred workers into a Dopolavoro and set off a series of mass clashes and conflicts as a compact force.

We can must arrive at taking over local Dopolavoros and holding them. This doesn't mean we will immediately strip them of their Fascist label. But these organizations are in fact working in a spirit of opposition to fascism or internally are still maintaining democratic organizational forms. We must join the Dopolavoro and create Communist cells in it.

We must not forget that the Dopolavoro also can act as a cover for Party cells, union groups, etc. This possibility is tied to the possibility we have of creating autonomous organizations in many places. When it is possible to have an autonomous organization, we must create it. There are cases in which something has been done, but these cases are still too few.

At a certain point, these organizations are forced to adhere to the Dopolavoro. What should they do? They must discuss things and resist to the very end. But if there's no way out (join the Dopolavoro or disband), then they must join and remain constantly tied to the masses. Indeed, these organizations can serve us in many cases as solid points of support for connecting up with other local Dopolavoros.

I don't have time to dwell on other subjects which I should have touched on and which necessarily must be put off for the discussion period. I think, however, I have succeeded in giving a picture of the possibility we have of exploiting the Dopolavoro and of the necessity of exploiting it in the broadest possible way.

lecture 7

Corporativism[1]

WE SHALL devote two lessons to the problem of corporativism. Normally, this subject would not warrant two lessons, but in this lesson we must acquaint ourselves with a discussion that has taken place on this subject in our Political Bureau.

This discussion goes to show that the problem of corporativism is more complex than it seems at first sight; it proves that differences of opinion and misunderstandings on the problem of corporativism can be found even among the Party's leading elements. This is why it is necessary to examine the question of corporativism more closely than usual, not limiting ourselves to saying (what in substance is true) that corporativism is nothing but a series of words, of slogans, with which fascism tries to cover up the class dictatorship of the most reactionary and chauvinistic strata of finance capital. This is substantially, but only partly, true. To limit ourselves to this means not getting a clear view of the whole problem; it means not seeing all of its aspects; it means overlooking the fact that corporativism is not only a propaganda tool, a demagogic slogan fascism uses for the masses, but is also a reality: corporativism is the organizational form fascism has given and is endeavoring to give to Italian society and especially to certain aspects of the activity of the state.

Fascism always has called itself corporative. But the word *corporativism* has not always had the same meaning. Fascism, we repeat, has always declared itself to be corporativism. You will find this repeated by Mussolini when he says that it's not enough for the fascist state to be totalitarian, but that it must be corporative as well. You will find the word *corporation* even in the first documents of the Fascist Party, in the party's first statute; but the reality that corresponds to this word is different in the different moments of fascism's development. Fascism wants to have one believe in its rational development and to pass off the latest measures as crowning an action which fascism has planned in its various moments of development.

Fascism must be refuted on this point. But in a certain sense corporativism can and must be viewed as crowning the action of the fascist organization of the state. What's more, we must bear in mind that in the international field the two concepts, *fascism* and *corporativism*, are generally thought of as equivalents today. Take countries where there's a typical fascist dictatorship—Germany and Austria, for example: you will find attempts there to create a corporative state. Corporativism is the watchword of Austrian and German fascism. Take countries where the fascist movement is still developing and has not yet taken power: one of its ideological and propaganda motifs is corporativism. Look at France, for example: the slogan *corporativism* is part of the propaganda arsenal of all the fascist groups. And this watchword *corporativism* is set up in opposition to the current organization of the state, to the current economic system. Corporativism is portrayed as a different kind of system. Look at England, a country where the fascist movement is not thriving to any great extent, but where it has had and may still have a certain growth. For various reasons, this is the fascist movement tied most closely to Italian fascism. Well, it too has as its basis the program of organizing corporativism; it proposes to reorganize England on corporative bases. In other countries, where there already is a fascist state and a tendency toward its fascistization, corporativism is one of the integral elements of the respective fascisms.

To this, another element must be added: there are movements which cannot yet be defined fascist, movements in which there is a current tendency to intervene in the economic field. But in these cases fascism interprets such interventions as corporativism, as an application of its principles. This is the case of Roosevelt, for example.

This shows us the great importance of studying the problems of corporativism and the necessity of stripping fascist propaganda of its cover, of demonstrating the reality of corporativism especially on the basis of the Italian experience.

Another point I want to touch on is the ideology of corporativism. Here, too, we must be careful. Corporativism is not indivisible, something that stands on its own logic, but is extremely varied and composite. Corporativism has many interpretations. In Italy, there is an interpretation which we could call "socialist," the interpretation made by *Problemi del lavoro.*[2] Here, corporativism is regarded as the realization of the principle of class collaboration in the field of the organization of the economy.

But there are other interpretations, several in the fascist camp itself. You know that there is an extreme current of thought—we'll call it a "far-leftist" current—that maintains that corporativism ought to be organized on the basis of proprietary corporations. According to this interpretation, the corporations should be owned by the factors of production. This is the thesis that Professor Ugo Spirito upheld at the Ferrara Conference,[3] a thesis that was fought by the majority. But this interpretation has been put forth since then. Even at the Ferrara Conference, Spirito was not censured outright. And this thesis still crops up now and then today; you will find it expounded and aired in little reviews.

This interpretation of corporativism shows how the concept of corporativism allows fascism to maneuver, inasmuch as it can cover any and all goods, even goods which can be considered "subversive"—for example, the idea of the proprietary corporation, which inevitably must lead to the conclusion that it is necessary to expropriate the capitalists.

This variety of interpretation is one of the problems that render the study of corporativism more difficult, for there is the risk of mistaking what one or another of the theoreticians of corporativism say for reality; there is the risk of mistaking what is said for what is done, what fascism says for what is the reality of Italian life.

What are the fundamental points? What was a guild in the Middle Ages?[4] It was an association of all those who plied the same craft—cobblers, tailors and so forth. The medieval guild therefore had a unitary nature since when it existed the capitalist system had not yet developed, the base of production was still constituted by the handicraft body and there was therefore no distinction between proletarians and capitalists. Thus, the guild was something different from what it is made out to be today.

Fascism depicts the corporation as the synthesis of two elements: the capitalist and the proletarian. This feature did not exist in the medieval guild. All of fascism's references to the medieval guild (they still are being made today, although they were more frequent in the early years) are meaningless. Today's reality is the reality of the capitalist regime, something very different from that of the Middle Ages; and not only of the capitalist regime, but of capitalism at a high stage of development in which the contradictions, the class struggles, have reached their highest point, and the problem of the destruction of the capitalist system is posed as a present-day task.

The second point is the collaborationist aspect of corporativism. Here we are dealing with what is really an essential and substantive element. In Italy, when the Fascists have spoken and speak of corporativism, they affirm the necessity of class collaboration and the necessity of eliminating the class struggle through collaboration. This is true not only in Italy but in all countries, anywhere corporativism stands out as a means of eliminating the class struggle. Hence, it is readily understood why the fascist unions called themselves syndical corporations at the [illegible] even though their nature was entirely different. At their founding congress, the fascist unions took the name *corporations* because boss and worker, capitalist and proletarian participated or, rather, could have participated in them. This guild-slanted interpretation of fascist trade-unionism is one of fascism's attempts to build something on the basis of its own corporative ideology.

But corporativism as class collaboration is not in the least an invention of fascism. It derives on the one hand from the extreme right-wing currents of socialism; petty-bourgeois, anti-Marxist currents that arose within the Second International. Furthermore, we find it in the right wing of the French socialist movement, which reproduced some elements of Proudhonism. It has a clear-cut reformist derivation, which is why one runs across *Problemi del lavoro*, for example, in the corporativist camp. And this also explains why some Socialist political exiles can be found on this terrain at certain moments; for example, at certain times you will find affirmations completely favorable to corporativism in *Avanti!*[5]

The second origin, or rather the second point of contact, of corporativism as class collaboration is found in Catholic social ideology. You know—and we shall see it more clearly when we speak of the Catholic movement—that in the encyclicals *Rerum novarum* and *Quadragesimo anno*[6] you will find quotations, passages, that correspond to the corporative propaganda of fascism. It's no accident that the Catholic Church and the Vatican substantially accept Italian corporativism, and that in Austria, where fascism is bound more closely to the Catholic Church than in Italy, fascism has immediately set about rebuilding the state apparatus on a corporative basis.

Class collaboration is a point we must underscore in the corporative ideology.

Insofar as its aim is to achieve class collaboration through a common organization of capitalists and proletarians, is corporativism feasible? The results in this field are telling. It is *not feasible.* I won't insist on this point; we've already demonstrated it throughout the course of fascism. We have seen that fascism's policy sharpens class conflicts rather than diminishing them. To a certain extent it succeeds in disguising these conflicts, but not in suppressing them; and, indeed, we will see them arise on the terrain of corporativism itself.

But there is also a second point, and it is this one that must be emphasized today. I mean to speak of corporativism as an attempt to create a new form of economic organization. Today, this is the most important point for fascism. The thing is not without meaning, not without a real justification. You will find this element if you examine corporative propaganda of the earliest period, but it was not predominant. It has made headway and has been brought into the foreground especially in recent times. This second element of corporativism, conceived as a new regime in opposition to the socialist regime but which at the same time transcends the capitalist regime, is dominant as of late. You will find this concept expressed in Mussolini's speeches. Before, he openly defended capitalist society, saying that the capitalist regime had a right to exist. He even used liberal arguments. Lately, instead, you can see this new element arise. At a certain moment, Mussolini is unsure if this crisis is "a crisis in the system or of the system"; at another given moment, he declares that the crisis is of the system and that the capitalist system must be transcended. Statements of this kind are being made more or less openly. You will find the most open one in the speech to the factory workers of Milan,[7] but you will also find them in a series of fascist documents; for example, in the motion the Superior Council of Corporations approved on December 13. There you will find this formulation: "The National Council of Corporations is an instrument which, under the aegis of the state, effects the integral, organic and unitary discipline of the forces of production with a view to increasing the wealth, political might and well-being of the Italian people."

This is a most important affirmation. You will find it in a Milan speech although somewhat toned down. But what dominates is the concept that the integral, unitary organization of the economy is brought about by means of the corporations. This is the concept that has prevailed as of late in fascism's corporative propaganda.

You will find this concept again in the speech delivered to the annual conclave of the regime in 1934. The concept is repeated, the idea of the "crisis of the system" is accentuated. Once this has been acknowledged, says Mussolini, then it is necessary to work toward another system, our system: "the economy, disciplined, strengthened and harmonized, with a view above all to a collective utility of the producers themselves (entrepreneurs, technicians, workers), through corporations created by the state, which represents the whole—including, that is, the other side of the phenomenon: the world of consumption."

Here the concept appears in an even more complete, more

elaborate form. Why have these statements been cropping up in the past few years? Because they are the years of the crisis. There is an objective basis to the development of fascism's corporative propaganda from propaganda of class collaboration to propaganda for a new system; a system that is not even presented as organized capitalism, but as an organized economy which breaks with capitalism too.

There is a real basis to all this: fascism has come up against a very grave economic crisis, a crisis that has had repercussions on the country's whole economy and has led to modification of class relations. What has fascism done to attenuate the crisis of capitalism? As we have seen, it has pursued a policy that has favored the concentration of capital, a policy that has led to the predominance of finance capital throughout the country's economy. We have seen how fascism's policy favors the process of concentration and how its whole policy is aimed at strengthening the positions of finance capital. This is the real basis of corporativism, the real basis of the most recent aspects of corporative propaganda and ideology.

This real basis is not limited to Italian fascism alone. It is common to Italian fascism and to that of a good many other countries. In this sense, fascist corporativism is not original: it is nothing but an attempt to present a more complex, more organic formulation of that which is being presented in every country as a way out, as a way of overcoming the current situation; it is nothing but a way of formulating the capitalistic attempts at so-called "planning." You know that plans are being talked about everywhere. And the bourgeois theorists, the bourgeois economists, never tire of speaking of the need to plan the economy, to overcome anarchy by organizing production. The question has various aspects, but at bottom it boils down to only one thing. On the one hand, we see the bewilderment of some groups of the bourgeoisie in the face of the present crisis, in the face of their fear of a proletarian revolution. On the other, we see a mask being used to try to disguise the paths by which the bourgeoisie intends to deal with the crisis: by organizing the supremacy of finance capital throughout the country's economy, the supremacy of the strong over the weak; by organizing, through a series of measures, the offensive against the working class, against the laboring masses. This is the reality; this is the basis of the motives for the ideology and propaganda of economic organization.

They say they want to organize the economy according to a plan. Is this possible? You know that we answer on principle and demonstrate that it is impossible. Why is it impossible? It is impossible because a plan can be introduced only if the principle on which the capitalist economy is founded has been destroyed. The capitalist economy is anarchic, not because capitalists aren't men of good will, but because it is based on profit. Only after a revolution that destroys the principles on which capitalist society is founded can planning be spoken of. To plan the economy *is not possible* otherwise. In the Soviet Union, the economy can be planned precisely because the capitalist regime has been overthrown and the working class is organizing its economy on new principles.

In what do the planning attempts in the field of the bourgeois economy consist? They correspond to an intervention by the decisive, strongest strata of capitalism; they correspond to the intervention of finance capital in the organizing of the country's economy through the state apparatus, the state machine. The attempts at a program of capitalist planning are nothing but the formulation in propaganda terms of what has taken place under the pressure of the crisis; they are nothing but a formulation in terms of social demagogy of what is happening in all the great imperialist countries, where finance capital is extending its rule and trying to exclude the others.

Are the fundamental conflicts and contradictions being overcome through the attempts at planning? Not by a long shot! They are being accentuated. The basic contradiction between the developing forces of production and the constantly declining capacity to consume is being accentuated. The other contradictions are being accentuated too. The struggle among capitalist groups is being accentuated by the general spread of the great monopoly trusts. Free competition, which is the origin of the anarchy of production, apparently is suppressed, but is being reproduced on a vaster scale inside the individual monopolies and among them.

What elements of a planned economy exist in Italy? Here

again caution should be exercised in making assertions. I think it is incorrect to affirm that state intervention is tending to limit the development of the forces of production in Italy. Even the law that sets a limit on the opening of new factories doesn't represent an intended curb; it is nothing but a state intervention designed to strengthen certain elements. In fact, except for a handful, all the applications for new plant openings have been approved. This law represents nothing but the rule, through an organization that is in the hands of the state, of the groups that have a dominant position and are trying to make these positions stronger and stronger. This is not an economic plan. The state isn't saying don't make any more shoes because no one is buying them and they can't be sold. With its intervention, the state wants the shoes produced by the big capitalists to be paid for by banks right from the very moment these new factories are opened. You will find such intervention in industry and agriculture: in agriculture, not only in the formation of consortium, but in the very organization of the "wheat battle," which in other ways tends to favor the interests of the strongest elements in agriculture and to establish their dominion over the intermediate and weakest ones. Planning comes down to this: on the one hand, creation of new monopolies, strengthening of preexisting ones, guarantees of predominance in the field of production; and on the other, organization of the offensive against the working masses.

These laws that turn up every so often in the Italian press, the founding of a corporative consortium of cotton manufacturers for a standard type of yarn or fabric—what do these things in fact mean? Do they mean that production is being organized in a way that is more advantageous to the great mass of consumers? Absolutely not. These measures tend to drive out of production a series of small textile mills which, not being able to install a large amount of new machinery, of new looms, cannot manufacture these standard goods. The intervention of the state (the intervention of the strongest monopoly groups) serves this purpose; it serves to reinforce, through state law, the elements that rule supreme in the Italian economy.

But there is also the other element to which we have referred: the state intervenes to bolster the offensive against the working masses. In no other country has the state intervened as it has in Italy in order to cut wages, to an extent and with the means which are well known to you. Is this perhaps an organizing of the capitalist economy? It's clear that this is nothing but an offensive against the working masses. In this sense, new factors exist, factors linked to the third element of corporativism, which I will now discuss.

What has fascism been able to accomplish in this direction? It would be a mistake to state flatly that it hasn't been able to accomplish anything. First of all, it has achieved a strengthening of the offensive against the working masses; second, it has been able to organize the offensive not only against the working masses, but also against sectors of the petty and middle bourgeoisie which have been jostled and shoved aside by the big producers, the big industrialists whose position is predominant. But there is still another element: has fascism been able to lessen the consequences of the crisis for those who make up these big monopolies? Without doubt, fascism has succeeded here. For this reason, in examining the aspects of the crisis, in examining the curve of production, one must never forget the value of this fact. This fact has made it possible not only to launch the offensive against the working masses and to drive out the weakest elements, whom Mussolini tells frankly, "You must go and break your bones"; but also to lessen the consequences of the crisis for these monopoly groups. Thus, in examining the development, the forms, the consequences of the crisis, one cannot fail to give consideration to corporativism seen in its second aspect; seen not as class collaboration, but as an element that is organizing the predominance of the highest strata of industry, of the banks—in a word, of finance capital.

Therefore, it is not a question of a new system, but of the capitalist system at its highest stage, at the stage of imperialism. Italian imperialism has a more marked character than that of the other countries. What we say about Italian imperialism is true: it is one of the weakest because it lacks raw materials, etc. But from the point of view of its organization and structure, no doubt it is one of the most largely developed.

We come now to the third element. So far, we have seen two elements: the element of collaboration and the element of organization. The third element is this: *corporativism is not conceivable, is inconceivable, without the fascist state*; corporativism is inconceivable without the Fascist Party; it is inconceivable without the dismantling of the whole system of democratic liberties. You will find clear, forthright affirmations on this point in the documents of fascism. Here, for example, is a commentary in *Gerarchia*[8] on the Ferrara Conference, an article of no particular consequence which attempts to outline the pillars of the corporative system: "Point one: any scientific elaboration of the corporative organization cannot depart from the historic fact of the Fascist revolution and of the political conception that is its soul."

This affirmation has a precise meaning, with which we agree: corporativism is not conceivable without fascism. Take the corporative propaganda of all fascisms everywhere. You will always find it tied to the polemic against parliamentarianism, against the principles of '89; you will find it tied to the struggle to abolish the democratic liberties, to dismantle democracy.

This also explains why corporativism was organized late in Italy. Corporativism was organized only after all the democratic liberties had been liquidated, when the workers had been deprived of all representation, when all the political parties had been destroyed, when trade-union freedom, freedom of the press, freedom of assembly had been liquidated, when every possibility of expressing oneself had been eliminated. This was the political premise of corporativism. Corporativism is inconceivable without the existence of fascism as a political dictatorship, without the existence of the Fascist Party as the instrument for exercising this dictatorship. We can see how the Fascist Party is arbiter in the corporations. Even if the corporations had some importance, they would not be able to do anything not approved by the Fascist Party. Along with the 268 representatives of the employers there are 268 representatives of the workers and, flanking them, 137 representatives of the technical experts and 66 of the Fascist Party. Even if the workers' representatives were truly such and not tools in the hands of the industrialists, we can see how the party still has ensured the predominance of the entrepreneurs. How was the corporative principle organized in Italy? It was organized through a long process, with turns, twists, experiments. The Fascist Party, fascism, always talked of corporativism. But the attempt at enactment dates back only to April 3, 1926, when the necessity of creating a Ministry of Corporations and a Corporative Central Committee was brought up, but the corporations themselves were not organized. Thus, we had a paradoxical situation from 1926 to 1934, until today: we had corporativism, there was a Ministry of Corporations, but there were no corporations.

Nonetheless, state intervention in economic life was effected; it was effected through the Ministry of Corporations and the various ministries of the economy. Legislative enactment has come about only in the most recent years, in the latest period of the economic crisis, at a time when fascism has been confronted with particular difficulties tied to the transition from the low-point of the crisis to a depression—a transition made without a drop in unemployment, without any improvement in the conditions of the working class. This situation has called for stepped-up pressure on the working masses and measures to guarantee the positions of the ruling groups. This is why particularly in the past few years we have seen greater intervention by the state in this field. We have seen the creation of big financial institutions which centralize the banking system; we have seen bail-out measures for faltering banks, interventions of which Mussolini is not afraid to say openly that "they have cost us billions." At this moment, the corporations have entered the field of legislation and we have corporativism with corporations. At this moment, the economic policy of fascism, the organization of the supremacy of finance capital in the country's economic life, has reached the highest point.

All this demonstrates that the corporative regime is organized on the basis of real relations. It is nothing but the demagogic and propaganda cover for the real relations that have grown out of the economic crisis; it is nothing but a cover for real conflict among the various groups of capitalists. This also explains the differences between Italian corporativism and that of the other countries.

In German corporativism, we can see a big difference from the structural point of view. Its structure is different in that trade unions do not exist as such in German corporativism. We have already explained why there are no unions as such in Germany. Italian corporativism was organized after fascism had unleashed the offensive against the working class to destroy its organizations, an offensive which led to a retreat of the positions of the working class. Corporativism in Germany, instead, is tied to a movement which took power without destroying the trade unions, so that to maintain these unions would have been much more dangerous than it had been in Italy. Italian fascism argues with German fascism, saying that German corporativism is not corporativism inasmuch as it doesn't have unions. In reality, there are no unions for class reasons. The strength of the German working class is very great, and a trade-union organization would involve enormous risks, much larger than in Italy.

But note that in Italy, too, there was a tendency to liquidate the unions in changing over to the corporations. This tendency made itself felt and was due to the fact that in this period, in '32, '33, factory workers in the party were tending to put up resistance within the unions themselves under the pressure of the economic crisis. There was this tendency, there were proposals to liquidate the unions, proposals which came from some of the fascist groups tied most closely to the industrialists. The liquidation of trade-unionism would have been favorable for the industrialists; even as they are now organized, the unions still represent a class organization which the workers can exploit. For this, there arose this tendency—for clarity's sake we'll call it "far-right"—whose aim was to liquidate the unions.

We overrated this tendency. If you read an article on this subject by Comrade Nicoletti in *Stato Operaio*,[9] you'll see that he thought the unions were done for. But fascism couldn't liquidate the unions because opposition to this arose inside the Fascist Party itself. The liquidation of the unions would have made the problem of control more acute. By liquidating the unions, fascism would have shattered one of the tools it needed, and may still need for some time to come, for controlling the masses. Another side, as we have seen, was represented by Spirito, who was inclined to favor state intervention as a means of eliminating privileges. This tendency, of course, could be found only in speeches and in the newspapers.

The line that was taken was that of organizing the corporations while retaining the unions. But are the unions represented in the corporations? We have to see. It is an important problem. Is there a difference between the unions and the corporations? Some comrades say the difference is only one of degree, that the corporations are the continuation of the unions. This point of view is mistaken. The difference is one of *quality*, not only of quantity and degree. The point is not only that the state intervenes more; the point lies elsewhere: the unions are mass organizations, the corporation a bureaucratic organism. It is fascism that says the difference is only one of degree. But we must look at the reality: in the unions there is the mass which, more or less, in one way or another, can make its voice heard; the corporations, instead, are a bureaucratic organism which the workers do not reach.

How are the corporations organized? What is their structure? What are their functions according to law and how do they work? You know that there are twenty-two corporations: a first group comprises an agricultural cycle of production, a second group an industrial cycle of production, the third the service activities. These corporations range from the cereals corporation, which is the first, to the tourism corporation, which is the last. For a long time it was debated: should the corporations be organized by trade or by product? This was not an idle discussion. What would have been the meaning of corporations organized on the basis of trades? The representatives of the workers and of the bosses would still have been face to face in them; class conflicts would still have arisen. The organization on a product basis, instead, is the organization of the representatives of the bosses and of the workers of all the trades that contribute to the production of a given product. In the cereals corporation, for example, there are the representatives of the bosses and of the workers of the flour mills, bread bakeries, pastry industry, grain trade, agricultural experts, etc. In the horticulture and floriculture corporation, you will find the representatives of the citrus-fruit growers, of the manufacturers of extracts and even of the chemical industry.

There is a difference between the two kinds of corporations. Why did fascism choose this path? It is explained very well in speeches and articles: organization on a trade basis would have meant that class conflicts would have been brought into the corporations, that the bosses and workers still would have been face to face. This would have meant that the corporations would have been nothing more than the organ of collaboration between two class syndical organizations.

In the product-by-product setup, a different element comes to the forefront: the intervention of the strongest groups to impose their will on the weakest. What problems are discussed in the corporations? If you take a look at the newspapers, you will see that the only things discussed are problems regarding the relations among the different groups of industrialists and the problems of organizing production. Relations between bosses and workers are not discussed, although in time they, too, no doubt will be treated. But it is a fact that in choosing this path, fascism indicated that the nature of the corporations was meant to mark a sharp break between unions and corporations.

What is the structure of a corporation? It is based on "equal" representation of the employers and of the employees, of the technical experts and of the Fascist Party. This "equality" is only an illusion. As we already have seen, even if the employees' representatives (who are chosen bureaucratically from among the union officials) were truly representatives of the workers, the upper hand would still be given to the bosses by the representatives of the Fascist Party and the technical experts. There is only one president of the corporations: Mussolini. This fact alone shows the predominance of the political factor in the organization of the corporations.

What are the corporations' functions according to law? They have functions of "coordinating and organizing productive activities," they have a consultative function and a mediating function. Article 44 says that the corporations are empowered to promote, encourage and support all initiatives aimed at improving production. With regard to their consultative functions, the organizations can offer their opinion on all questions concerned with production. As for their mediating functions, instead, attempts to effect conciliation in disputes between workers and entrepreneurs are entrusted to the corporations.

The question of whether the corporations can make laws has been discussed a good deal. Bottai[10] is one who upheld this point of view. He said the corporations must also have legislative powers (that is to say, they ought to set themselves up as a parliament). In reality, nothing has been done. And all this indicates how meager the reality of corporativism is when compared to fascism's campaign.

As for the functioning of the corporations, there's still little we can say. So far, three corporations have met: textiles, livestock and fishing, and transport. What questions were discussed? Let's see. Reports and articles in *Lavoro fascista*[11] show that very violent discussions took place, not between bosses and workers, but between individual industrialists. There had been an example of this earlier in the marble industry in Carrara, where there had been a fight with the cement manufacturers. The marble producers were demanding that every house in Italy be made of marble so that they could sell their output. The cement manufacturers were against this, and so a struggle took place. In the meeting of the livestock corporation, the decision was made to form a committee to draft a bill regulating cattle imports, a vote was passed to review the regulations governing slaughterhouses and meat and fish markets, and, finally, a request was made for collaboration in defining what ought to come under the trade of *tuna* (!).

In another corporative meeting, it was decided to form a single obligatory consortium for the production of Parmesan cheese. This is something new; it is a step ahead in the setting up of monopoly.

Thus, we see that the whole activity of the corporations boils down to asking the state to intervene with protective measures, tariffs, etc., and at the same time we see state intervention to create new monopolies. The meetings are held behind closed doors, the industrialists squabble and the government decides.

Before closing, I must touch on a final element. What can the corporations create? What value can they have? Can they have a real value tomorrow in regulating production over and above the monopolies? It's plain they can do something. Let's remember the past, the war years, the creation of the committees for industrial mobilization that organized the economy for war purposes. The corporations can have these functions. From this point of view, the corporative structure is the groundwork for an organization of production keyed to war.

In conclusion, the basic points to remember are the following: 1) the corporative regime is a regime that is inseparable from total political reaction, from the destruction of every democratic liberty; 2) the corporative regime corresponds to an advanced economic stage and is a form through which finance capitalism seeks to strengthen its positions in the country's economy; 3) the state form must be totalitarian so as to force the large working masses under its control; 4) the corporations are an instrument for suppressing any attempt by the working masses to liberate themselves; 5) the corporations are an instrument for the ideological propaganda of class collaboration; 6) hiding behind the mask of an "anti-capitalist" ideology, the corporations represent the most reactionary organization of the capitalist regime.

lecture (cont.) 7

Our Policy Toward the Corporations

LAST time, we saw what the corporations are; and we tried to explain not only what they are in the propaganda and demagogy of fascism, but what they are in reality—as a model of Italian political life and of the organizational structure of the fascist dictatorship. We saw: 1) that the corporations are an organization that is part and parcel of the system of political reaction, of the curtailment of every democratic liberty and of every possibility of the workers to organize; 2) that they are a form that has been adopted in the current moment of state action to ensure the predominance of finance capital in Italian economic life; 3) that state intervention is carried out systematically through the corporative system to ensure the positions of finance capital and to permit it to launch an offensive against the working class; 4) that the corporations are an instrument of collaborationist propaganda; 5) and, finally, that they are a framework through which those who hold the dominant positions in the Italian economy are trying to continue their policy undisturbed while hiding behind a cover of anti-capitalist phraseology and diverting the masses from the struggle.

How is the problem of the attitude of the working class toward the corporations posed? And what must be our Party's position? The two things are not unrelated. We shall therefore examine in general the position that the working class and the workers' movement must have on this problem.

This problem cannot be resolved properly if its solution is not based on a correct position of principle, on a political examination of the relation of forces existing in the country, on a correct solution of the tactical problems of the workers' movement and of the Party.

Let's begin by seeing what social democracy's positions are toward the corporations. You will find a complete exposition in your notebook on social democracy. In social democracy there are three currents of thought (which, in substance, boil down to two). The first current seemed to prevail at a certain moment in Italian social democracy, and to become the official or semi-official position. Then this situation changed, in part owing also to our Party's active intervention. In a word, this current was represented by *Problemi del Lavoro*, by Caldara and by others who followed him.[1]

They assumed a positive attitude of consent, a collaborationist attitude, toward the corporations. What does positive attitude mean? It means regarding the institution of the corporations as a step fascism has taken on a path which is favorable to the working class. This is the broadest justification that can be given for the positions of Rigola and Caldara. But other, more important ones can be found if you read Rigola's articles and those of the followers of the Caldara group (published in the Paris edition of *Avanti!*). For example, take a look at an article published in *Avanti!* and signed "K." It says: "In Italy, we find ourselves in a one-front situation of necessity. We see no possibility of doing work, of expressing an opinion. There's no way out. We must cling to the corporations in order to intervene in the country's political life."

There are two arguments made here. We find that the first is repeated in other forms even by the official leaders of the Socialist party, in some articles by Pietro Nenni and in a series of other writings. These arguments consist in saying: if we get to the bottom of Rigola's and Caldara's positions on the corporations, we will see they mean that fascism effectively is transcending capitalism, is making progress toward a noncapitalistic system of production, toward socialism.

How are these arguments presented? They are presented in such a form as to possibly mislead not the masses, because these arguments generally do not reach them, but elements who are rather accustomed to discussing these problems.

We know that according to one of the positions of Marxism, the elements of socialist society mature within capitalist society. This Marxist affirmation is repeated by Lenin and Stalin and all orthodox voices. This affirmation is one of the factors that guarantees the necessity of the overthrow of capitalism. Even in the past, leaders of the workers' movement, basing themselves on this affirmation, reduced Marxism to a revolutionary fatalism or stated that the problems posed in the actual moment were being resolved by German capitalism. You can find this position in every moment and in every country. You will find it later on especially in the Economists of Russia. If you study throughly the only Marxist we had in Italy, Antonio Labriola,[2] you will find traces in him of this fatalism and a tendency to regard the bourgeoisie's development in the actual moment, the things it does, the manifestations of imperialism, the struggle to subdue other countries, the struggle for expansion, as things we must accept because they are leading us towards socialism.

It was on this basis that Labriola slid to the point of legitimizing the Italian expansion in Africa. (The position he took in the famous interview of 1904 is well known.) We must support this expansion, he said, because it is bringing us nearer to socialism. You can see how there no longer is anything Marxist about this position. Here you can see how from a correct position one moves over to plainly incorrect positions, forgetting the present-day conditions that have been studied, forgetting that socialism is built on the basis of these conditions and that the struggle must be founded on real conditions; and one says that capitalism itself, driven by its own economic conditions, must pose and resolve the problem of socialism.

This is the position of Rigola, of Caldara; and, at bottom, it is also the original ideological position of Pietro Nenni. You see how Caldara presents the system of corporativism. He presents it and justifies it with this fundamental affirmation: the bourgeoisie is realizing a part of socialism by means of this system. This is the same as asserting that finance capital's dominance of the country's economic life is the realization of a part of socialism. You can see what socialism means in this formulation: Caldara confuses the objective bases of the socialist revolution with the socialist movement. This is his fundamental error. Today, the capitalist economy is laying the foundations of the future system, but it is not realizing socialism. Caldara goes so far as to transform something into its opposite, to transform the most reactionary and most complete dictatorship of the bourgeoisie into its opposite—the dictatorship of the working class. With the formulations, "Socialism has moved out of the propaganda phase and has entered present-day life," and, "The bourgeoisie has appropriated just the amount of socialism it needed," etc. [some quotations from pp. 18-19 of the notebook on social democracy are not given here — *Transcriber*], not only is corporativism given justification, but the political formula "Nothing outside the state"—this formula that is producing the oppression of the workers—is presented as socialism! This is Caldara's position. You can find it in the articles and comments he wrote on the setting up of the corporations.

But Rigola goes even further. Rigola is freer in his actions. He has been on the path of open collaboration with fascism since 1927. He says something more: that the corporations can be accepted, that they are good and useful, provided liberty is added to the corporations. In a word: if the corporations were what they are, but if they were also democraticallly organized, then we would have the realization of socialism. This is, as it were, the mathematical formula of this current: corporations + liberty = socialism. At a certain moment, this was the formula of *Avanti!* and of the Socialist leadership. [At this point, Comrade Ercoli quotes several passages from p. 20 of the notebook on social democracy to indicate Nenni's position—*Transcriber.*]

There developed a rather ample propaganda on this basis in the period right after the corporations were instituted, carried even further by the right-wing elements in the Socialist Party and by the neo-socialists in France. The formula was: add liberty to corporativism and you will have socialism. Rigola intensified his collaboration with fascism on this basis; Caldara offered to collaborate within the structure of the corporative regime on this basis. And, at a certain moment, the Socialist Party was moving toward this position. This tendency of the Socialist Party was broken by our Party, which did all it could to break it.

Some comrades may empirically pose the following problem: wouldn't it have been better for us to have let this tendency take its course so as to expose the Socialist Party more easily? This way of looking at the problem would be mistaken. This is a way of looking at the problem as propagandists, not as political movers. If the Socialist Party had openly gone over to collaboration with fascism, it would have been a blow to the workers' movement: a blow whose importance should not be overrated, and which would have been countered, but which would have been quite considerable all the same. It would have led part of the masses onto the terrain of corporativism. We joined with the Socialist Party, we made the united-front pact, and we thus averted this blow.

Do you see what are the roots of social democracy's incorrect position? You can find a whole series of mistaken positions of principle, of mistaken policy positions. Read all of Rigola's, Caldara's and Nenni's articles on the corporations. You will always find a completely negative underlying judgment of the possibility of the development of revolutionary struggles. Caldara says that the populace is becoming conservative; that thousands and thousands of working-class militants are in prison, but that the people either do not remember them or regard them as deluded visionaries. This is a political error; the former was an error of principle. Then there are the tactical errors: we find ourselves in a situation of necessity; we must seize on something in order to intervene in the life of the country. This something supposedly would be the corporations. At first sight, this position seems to have something in common with ours when we say that we must intervene in the country, exploit fascist legality, the legal possibilities, in order to get the masses moving. But you can clearly see how the two positions are different: our position looks only to the development of the struggle of the masses, to revolution; Caldara's position looks to collaboration with the bourgeoisie, to the terrain on which the bourgeoisie is to be found—in a word, to the fascist dictatorship. Our tactics look forward, theirs look backward. The difference between these two positions is illustrated magnificently by Lenin and by Stalin when they speak of the differences between revolutionary and reformist tactics.

Briefly, on our position, our Party took a position on corporativism right from the first moment with an appeal that appeared in the December 1933 issue of *Stato Operaio*.[3] This appeal contains formulations regarding the principles on which corporativism is based, and determines our policy position. It defines corporativism as a form of the rule of fascism, of the most reactionary, most chauvinist strata of finance capital, etc. In this appeal, the revolutionary way out of the current situation is contraposed to the way out the Fascists propound—the way of fascist corporativism. This, however, is only a propagandistic contraposition. Our position consists: in determining our stand on corporativism, declaring ourselves irrevocably opposed to it, and our stand on the character of the corporative organization, defining its reactionary class character; and in acting on a terrain which enables us to tie up with the masses and develop a broad mass movement against fascism.

Through partial struggles, we have to make the movement of the masses vaster and vaster. The Party must know how to raise the right slogans, suited to the Italian political situation: slogans which must direct the masses toward the shattering of the fascist legality, not stopping simply with partial demands. This objective, that is to say the shattering of the fascist legality, must enable us to go on to activity of a higher nature: to go from the smallest demands, those of most immediate concern to the workers, to the fight for shop stewards, union representation, etc., and on up to the calling of strikes. This is our path. Furthermore, we must fight for the application of the forty-hour week without a pay cut, fight against the reduction of wages, and go on to demand and fight for trade-union freedom. If the movement develops, the problem of raising slogans of a more advanced political nature becomes a problem of immediate character. But this must be done according to the circumstances, and we will speak about this in the discussion period.

A few words on the last discussion.

Its limits and point of departure were represented by the

claim that the Party ought to put the demand for freedom to elect worker representatives in the corporations at the center of its agitation. The discussion involved this demand and all the arguments invoked to support it.

It's clear the Party cannot accept, and must reject, this demand. What arguments are used to support it and how can we respond? Let's see.

What are, in fact, the relationships between the fascist unions and the corporations? The difference between the unions and the corporations is a difference of quality: the unions are mass organizations, the corporations are bureaucratic organs. Some comrades say that corporativism is the continuation of fascist syndicalism, or that the corporations are a completion of the fascist unions. This way of presenting the problem is incorrect; this is how the Fascists try to portray it. The corporations brake the movements of the masses.

In this regard, I could cite a series of examples. When the struggle of the masses develops inside the fascist unions, the matter is remanded to the corporations for settlement. The agitation is ended. If a comrade is not found who is able to carry it ahead, everything ends there. When the delegation is made to go to Rome, that's the end of it. There have been cases like this everywhere. This first position, namely, that the corporations complete the unions, is incorrect.

A second argument that is made consists in exposing the contradiction between what the corporations should be and what they are in reality. Today, we are entering a new phase. Before, it was said the organization would be based on equal representation. If this organization existed—so the argument goes—there would be the objective possibility of working on this basis, not equal, but democratic. But the workers' representatives are not workers; they are representatives of the bosses and of the Fascist Party. Presumably, we should say this: fascism is not keeping the promises it made on the corporations and is merely creating them as a bureaucratic structure.

Is this distinction true? First of all, it would be necessary to understand in what way fascism is different today from what it said it intended to be; to see which theme of fascist propaganda should be taken as a term of comparison. We know there were three conceptions of corporativism: 1) integral corporativism, that of the proprietary corporation; 2) corporativism implying the disbandment of the unions; 3) corporativism existing side by side with the unions.

What is the true corporative ideology? In reality, a corporative ideology does not exist. There are fragments of different ideologies: collaborationist, anti-capitalist, reactionary. None of these can be separated from the others, and there's nothing today that can be presented as something new. There is no leap; there's a logical development.

What is there to the proposition of pure corporativism? This is the most dangerous proposition. This proposition is the key to answering the question if, for the workers, corporativism represents progress compared to what fascism has been so far; if there are greater chances than in the past of defending the interests of the working class.

But to ask this question means accepting part of the fascist propaganda. To affirm this proposition means taking what the Fascists say about the corporative regime as true, as correct. Corporativism does not represent a new form in which the working class can make its voice heard and further its own interests. By insisting on underscoring the character of corporativism, one ends up by accepting it, at bottom, as something that is not all bad. One starts out by saying: corporativism is being realized in this way or that way. And ends up by saying: if corporativism were different from the way it actually is, etc. . . .

Can corporativism be organized in a different way? Can it become a terrain of struggle? Obviously not. This idea can be found in fascist propaganda and demagogy, but when we go from there to the reality of things, we run up against corporativism as it actually is.

The third problem is politically the vastest. It is said: previously Italian society was organized on the basis of parliamentary institutions. Today, parliament no longer exists, the period of parliamentarianism is over, capitalist society is being organized on different bases. Why shouldn't we take the same positions toward corporativism that we used to take toward parliament?

We were opposed to parliament, too, but we still entered it. We should do likewise with the corporations.

This is the typical doctrinaire argument. Apparently correct. Based on this affirmation, we can be accused of abstentionism. How do things really stand? The point is that the comrades who reason like this are simplifying reality and reducing it to a scheme.

First of all, we're not always against parliamentarianism. On principle, we are for soviets; but there are Communist parties that do raise the demand for parliament—for example, the Bulgarian, Rumanian and Yugoslav parties. This comes about under particular conditions when this demand is felt most strongly by the masses and when, especially, the character of the revolution is bourgeois-democratic.

But why do we enter parliament? Lenin said: "Until we are able to dissolve the bourgeois parliament and every other kind of reactionary institution, we must work inside them." Does this apply to corporativism? Yes, if we stop here. But Lenin continues: "Because the workers are in them, the masses are in them." Lenin never said to enter all the bourgeois institutions. He said to enter all the institutions where the masses can be found. Lenin's position on parliament assumes that parliament is, in a certain sense, a mass organization, a tribune to which the masses' eyes are turned, a tribune to which the masses lend an ear.

This is the criterion of differentiation, the line of demarcation between union and corporation, between parliament and corporation. To a greater or lesser degree, parliament is always a result, a point of arrival, a revolutionary conquest of the masses, a conquest of the bourgeois-democratic revolution. What masses make the bourgeois-democratic revolution? The masses of proletarians, of semi-proletarians, of peasants. This is why parliament must be seen as something that is tied to these masses. Take even the most reactionary of parliaments, the Duma, and you will see that the masses were tied to it since it was a remnant of a revolutionary conquest, a tribune from which they expected the defense of their interests

But do the masses really look to the corporations? When a corporation meets to deliberate the introduction of new customs duties, to set up a consortium for Parmesan-type cheeses, are the masses listening? If it were a tribune from which one could speak, then we would take a different position.

But, then, is it true that the period of parliamentarianism is over?

There are fascist countries in Europe. In the whole world there are only three great democratic states. Fascist dictatorship is tending to become the dominant form of bourgeois dictatorship. But does this mean the path to parliament is closed? We have a typical example in Spain. In Spain, there was a fascist dictatorship of a special kind because Spain is a country where there are still many elements of the bourgeois-democratic revolution. However, Primo De Rivera's fascistic dictatorship was overthrown. By whom? By the struggle of the masses. The bourgeoisie sought to tie up with the masses precisely through the Constituent Assembly and parliament.

When we see what the corporations are, we understand at once that it is meaningless to compare them with parliament.

But some say that it's necessary to demand liberty in order to expose them. I repeat, this an error of doctrinairism. It is an error to read the newspapers for what the Fascists say in order to make this the basis of slogans. For example, I read an article on worker control in *Lavoro fascista.* What would worker control be in Italy today? A wage cut is attempted, the workers go to the head office, they meet with the industrialists, they meet with the Fascists, who frighten them and convince them that the limit has been reached. This alone is the prospect: instead of unleashing the class struggle, we would be leading the workers to collaborate. This is why what the C[ommunist] I[nternational] says is right: worker control is a correct slogan only in a revolutionary situation.

Some comrades say it is not dangerous to raise this demand since it cannot be realized. But the masses, comrades, do not mobilize for unrealizable objectives. To raise this demand means asking for a democratic reform of the fascist regime; it means asking, as Caldera does, for an infusion of liberty; it means launching not an immediate, but a transitional, political, slogan that corresponds to a democratization of the fascist regime.

What are our slogans at the present moment? This is the heart of the question. This problem is tied closely to an exact evaluation of fascism's influence on the masses, of the degree of development of the movement of the masses, of the prospects of fascism and of the Italian situation. If these three questions are not answered correctly, the gravest mistakes and a distortion of our Party line are possible.

What is fascism's influence on the masses? Does it have such influence that, for the masses, the corporative organization could become what parliament once was? This influence does not exist. Remember what parliament was? Everyone knows that the first thing people used to look at when they picked up the newspaper was the parliamentary report. And the bourgeois press was built on the parliamentary design; it devoted the front page to reports on parliament. Parliament was a tribune the whole country looked to. Fascism destroyed it precisely because it was a tribune for agitating the masses. Is there something similar to this in the corporations? Absolutely not. It's a mistake to believe that fascism's influence on the masses represents an adherence of the masses to the fascist regime, that the masses adhere to the fascist regime just as they adhered to the democratic regime. Among the masses, there is an ideological influence; there is an adherence to some fascist organizations which can satisfy certain needs of the masses. But there is no adherence on the part of the great masses to corporativism. At the very most, we can find groups of workers who say: let's see what corporativism will turn out to be. In Apulia, they say: the word is that the land must be given to the peasants; let's wait and see what corporativism does.

There's no doubt, for example, that at FIAT the workers are waiting to see what will be done with the Bedaux system.[4] It is possible to speak of fascism's influence in this sense. The masses adhere to some fascist institutions or, rather, approach them only insofar as these satisfy some of their immediate needs.

The terrain on which the Party must act is still that of immediate demands, of demands that can mobilize the masses. Tell a worker in Milan, "We have to fight for the forty-ho week without a wage cut, to fight against the reduction wages," etc., and you will be able to generate mass meeting protests, movements. Say, instead, "Let's send a delegation to the corporations," and no one will listen to you. They won't listen to you because this demand *does not correspond to the degree of fascism's influence on the masses.* The key to exposing fascism is represented by the *most elementary immediate economic demands, by the exploitation of the legal possibilities, by the agitation of the masses and the effort to lead them into the struggle.*

Is this all? No. Besides this, our Party must have political slogans; otherwise we would lapse into economism. We must have political demands. Which ones? These demands cannot but have a democratic content; the popular liberties cannot but dominate. What democratic demands can we raise?

lecture **8**

Fascism's Policy in the Countryside

THE SUBJECT we shall treat today is one of the broadest, most complicated and most difficult of all. In a single lesson, we must clearly depict the foundations of fascism's policy in the countryside. Many comrades have already heard this question discussed in the course on the Italian economy and in the course on our Party's policy. For them, this may be a repetition; for the others, instead, the subject will be more difficult. And this is why, given the extremely limited time at our disposal, I will try not to go into too many details so as not to make the lesson unduly heavy.

In this lesson I want to give a quick overall view of what fascism has done in the countryside, comparing this with what fascism has done throughout the country's economy. I will try to indicate briefly the political and social consequences of fascism's policy in the last few years—the years, that is, of the economic crisis—and to demonstrate how we must base ourselves on these results in order to determine our policy line in this field.

We will take a statement found on p. 4 of your notebook as a point of departure. That page says: "At present, the various strata of agricultural workers are reduced to a state of impoverishment that is growing worse each day at an increasing pace."

Is this statement correct? And to what extent is it correct?

How should this statement be interpreted? We must provide an answer to this.

First of all, we must avoid interpreting statements of this kind, whether they refer to the rural crisis or to fascism's policy in the countryside, as meaning that fascism's policy and the rural economic crisis are producing a general impoverishment of the rural population. To affirm this would be incorrect, incorrect because it's not true that the crisis is producing a general impoverishment of *all* rural strata. The crisis is causing the impoverishment *of certain rural strata* while at the same time it is strengthening others.

I cannot dwell at length on this issue. But, roughly speaking, you can visualize things in this way: in the countryside we find working peasants, wealthy peasants, usurers, banks. The crisis causes a drop in the price of farm products and forces the small and medium-scale farmers, who are unable to meet their operating costs, to take out loans. But who is it that makes the loan? If someone receives money, there also must be someone who gives it to him. The loan is made by a wealthier landowner or by a usurer or by a bank. When this phenomenon spreads, we always can clearly see its two sides: on the one hand, there is a part of the rural population that goes deeper and deeper into debt, that has larger and larger liabilities in its farms; on the other, there is a richer and richer strata that makes loans. By whom is the latter strata represented? We have already said it: by the wealthy peasants, by the usurers, by the banks. Even from this simple fact, you can discern the two sides of the problem: on the one hand the poor who are growing increasingly poor, and on the other the rich who are growing increasingly rich.

Taking the results of this fact, what do you see? You see that the poor and middle peasants, finding it impossible to pay off their debts, cannot keep going and must sell their land. But here, too, there are two sides to the question: if someone sells land, there also must be someone buying it. The poor peasant and the middle peasant, oppressed by taxes or debts, are forced to sell their land. But their land is bought by the one who has made loans to them· by the rich peasant, by the owner of a larger piece of land, by the usurer, by the bank, etc.

This is a very simple exemplification, but the phenomenon has much deeper aspects.

We have discussed it in relation to the crisis. Now let's see how the phenomenon presents itself in relation to fascism's policy in the countryside. Fascism began implementing its policy in the countryside before the outbreak of the economic crisis. It's true that there had been an agrarian crisis even earlier, but it assumed acute forms only in 1926 and 1927. It was in this period that there was the first big drop in the price of farm products.

It would be a mistake to accept the following proposition: fascism's policy in the countryside has led to an impoverishment of all peasants. This is not true. We must view things objectively, politically. To make an affirmation of this kind would mean saying that fascism has lost or is about to lose—but since this policy of fascism has lasted for years, no doubt one should say has lost—every possibility of having a mass base in the countryside, of having a political base of support. This is not true. Let's make even a summary study of those who supported fascism in the countryside. What has happened to these strata? Who today supports fascism in the countryside? No doubt, we can note a change. But this change does not mean in the least that the base on which fascism rests in the countryside has been wiped out. We have had a shift in the mass base, not the class base.

Who formed fascism's base in the countryside at the time fascism took power? If you take the figures on the classification of the Italian rural population, figures that refer to 1911 and 1921, you will find that fascism's official statistics, based on the censuses taken in those years, show an increase in the number of rural property owners—not only a general increase, but an increase in the number of small and medium-scale landowners. This refers to the period that goes from 1911 to 1921. But do you remember what came in this period? The war, with all its outgrowths and consequences. In the immediate postwar period, there was a trend toward the formation of new strata of small landowners.

Here, too, we must see the two sides of the phenomenon. To see only one side would be an error. There was a trend toward the formation of small landownership through land purchase;

and there was another tendency, one that was pushing in the direction of creating small landownership by means of expropriation, by means of seizures of land on the part of the peasants.

Why do I say we must be careful to see both sides? Because if there is a trend toward the purchase of land, then there is one kind of political situation. In this case, some poor- and middle peasant strata have grown "rich" and tend to solve the land problem by purchasing. This is the path of agrarian reform. What does this mean? It means that the movement aims at modifying property relations in the field of agriculture not through a revolutionary course of action, but through one which involves the buying of land by new strata of the peasantry. Some elements of this tendency existed, for example, in Emilia, where it was a rather widespread phenomenon not only in the hill country but on the plains as well.

But which of the two phenomena was more important in Italy as a whole? The way of reform or the way of revolution? There is absolutely no doubt that the revolutionary phenomenon was by far the more important. Impressive masses of the Italian peasantry were appropriating the land for themselves through revolutionary action. This trend toward the revolutionary seizingof land was a dominant social and political phenomenon compared to the tendency to purchase new land, to solve the land problem by means of agrarian reform.

What did fascism do in this situation? In which strata did it find support in the immediate postwar period? First of all it found support from the agrarian capitalists, who gave it its initial thrust. But the agrarian capitalists were not fascism's only base of support. What gave fascism a certain mass base in the countryside, especially in Emilia, was precisely the fact that it received support from several strata of middle peasants who had grown more or less wealthy at about that time and were trying to expand and enlarge their farms by buying more land.

Why did these strata turn to fascism? Because in the postwar situation they found themselves under pressure from the agricultural laborers' movement and the rural movement, which the Socialist Party was steering on an incorrect line—a line rejecting these strata from an alliance with the urban proletariat and the rural masses.

This drift toward fascism was accentuated by the tendency to try to increase one's wealth. In the provinces of Bologna and Ferrara, for example, you will find that not only middle strata but even some of the poorest strata adhered to fascism. You have to remember what a village is. It represents a form of society in which the class struggle had not yet developed. The class struggle develops very slowly in these villages. When one group moves in a certain direction, other groups, although different from the viewpoint of their social standing, take the same path. They take it because as debtors, employees, etc. they are dependent on the former. Class positions are not very sharply defined. The positions of the lawyer, of the notary, of the moneylender, are important because they determine shifts of elements who objectively are in contradiction with these positions. These are the paths by which fascism was able to gain ground in the countryside after the war.

At the same time, you know what fascism's original program was. You know it contained certain radical statements which later, it's true, were set aside. Fascism took a position of opposition to the revolutionary movement. An open position. A position which, I am inclined to say, was turned against the agricultural wage laborers' movement and the development of the revolutionary movement in the countryside even earlier than against the factory workers. This was the direction in which fascism struck its main blow: to prevent the growth and spread of the trend toward an agrarian revolution. And at this time it backed the path of agrarian reform.

If you look at the fascist publications of 1921, especially the newspapers of several zones of Emilia, you will see that fascism voiced its intention of creating new strata of small and medium-scale landowners in order to blunt the drive of the proletarian organizations. These new strata of landowners were to have arisen through the purchase of land.

We have looked briefly and rapidly at what rural fascism's objective base was at the time power was seized. What did fascism do in the countryside once it was in power? You are well aware of what fascism's policy was immediately after it had taken power. It was a policy which, while not undertaking a direct offensive against wages, was immediately geared to an open strengthening of the capitalists' positions; a policy which gave the capitalists a free hand in their affairs and in the economic life of the country; which favored the predominance of industrial capital, of banking capital, and which above all favored the growth of industry. In all our lessons, we have stressed that it is a mistake to believe that fascism has done nothing at all to develop Italian industry. After fascism took power, there was a strong development of industry both from the quantitative and from the technical and organizational viewpoint. This was the principal, the characteristic line of the fascist dictatorship's economic policy in its early years.

This policy prompted an immediate reaction in the countryside. Its effects were felt not in that it caused a complete loss of the mass base, but in that it created profound discontent in the countryside and—I should say—arrested, caused an arrest in the process of the formation of new strata of small and medium-scale landholders. This process came to a halt. It cannot be said that small landholding disappeared. But what phenomena do you have before your eyes? You can see a strengthening throughout the general economy of the positions of finance capital and industrial capital. The development of industry indirectly caused an impoverishment of the countryside not only for the fact that industry absorbed a large amount of the available capital, but also because fascism applied in favor of industry a fiscal policy directed against the working farmer.

This explains the oscillations of the rural strata, especially during the period of the Matteotti crisis. These were oscillations of the rural petty and middle bourgeoisie, frightened by the policy initiated by fascism right after taking power—a policy much different from what they had expected. Fascism's policy tended to strengthen the positions of other social strata—the bankers and capitalists—and not of the rural petty and middle bourgeoisie.

With this situation in mind, fascism got set to tackle the problem of its own agrarian policy. This problem was raised in full when the problem of creating the totalitarian state was posed.

We must not shut our eyes to what fascism has been able to accomplish with this policy; and we must not shut our eyes to certain results which have been obtained, results which we must study. It's a mistake just to laugh in the face of problems such as the "wheat battle," "comprehensive land reclamation," the "economic organization of agriculture," the "phasing out of day labor in agriculture." It's a big mistake. In each of these fields, realities, at times impressive realities, correspond to the slogans fascism has launched; realities tending to transform class relations in the Italian countryside. There are political consequences here that we must contemplate.

Which of fascism's general slogans shall we examine briefly? First of all the "wheat battle"; second, "comprehensive land reclamation"; third, the attempts to organize the agricultural economy (through the founding of the so-called consortiums); and then the policy of "phasing out day labor in agriculture," the policy of "domestic colonization." These are the principal points. We shall examine them briefly, not in depth.

Let's look at the "wheat battle." All of you know its aim, its objective. Fascism says the objective of this campaign is to raise wheat production in Italy, "to produce enough wheat for every Italian." In other words, they want—they say—for Italy, which has always been an agricultural country, to stop importing wheat for domestic consumption. This campaign is presented like this, simply and demagogically: "Every Italian must eat Italian bread. If we don't achieve this, we won't have enough bread to feed everyone if a war comes."

What does the "wheat battle" mean in reality? The "wheat battle" means that in order to produce more wheat the Italian agricultural economy must be quite thoroughly transformed. You know that there is not a large amount of uncultivated land in Italy. The little land that is untilled is such because large amounts of capital would be required to make it produce. It is unfertile land, land that maybe never has been worked. Therefore, to increase the production of wheat, it is necessary to shift the axis of the Italian agricultural economy. How has fascism done? Has it obtained results in this field? We can't say no! It has been able to increase the size of the wheat harvest appreciably. But how has this progress been achieved? It has been achieved in two ways. First of all, wheat is being grown today in almost every locality, even on land where the only things grown before were orchard crops, fruit trees, etc. There has been an expansion of the total farmland planted with wheat. But this is not the most important aspect. The most important aspect is represented by the fact that the average yield of wheat per hectare in Italy is much higher today than it was before. In Italy today, a hectare produces 14 quintals[1] on the average—a rather high average yield. Before, the average yield fluctuated between 10 and 11 quintals. Now, 14 quintals are produced, and to produce these 14 quintals something must have been done. Here we can begin to see what the question is. What does it mean to have harvested 14 quintals instead of 10? It means having worked the land more intensively, having used better machines or simply having used machines where only primitive tools were used before; it means having used more fertilizer. In a word, it means that more capital has been spent per hectare than was spent before.

We are moving here from economic to social and political grounds. We can see that to achieve the results of the "wheat battle" it has been necessary to put more capital per hectare into the cultivation of wheat. But the more capital that is spent to grow wheat, the higher the price is at which this wheat is sold; if not, larger amounts of capital would not be invested. So fascism has had to introduce a policy designed to keep the price of wheat high: it has introduced the import duty on wheat. The import duty on wheat is the most important part of the "wheat battle." Without the duty on wheat, the "wheat battle" is inconceivable. You know that the import duty on wheat has led to an enormous difference between wheat prices in Italy and prices on the world market. But there are also other forms in which the state intervenes to favor an increment of wheat production per hectare: bonuses for wheat farmers, competitions, special terms of credit for the use of fertilizers, etc. These, however, are subsidiary forms; the principal form is represented by the import duty on wheat.

Something more must be said on this subject in order to provide a more detailed view of the question. This is the most difficult point also as far as an explanation in common language is concerned. In any case, I shall try to make you understand it.

Don't think that 14 quintals per hectare is the yield obtained throughout Italy. It is not. A hectare does not yield 14 quintals throughout Italy. Fourteen quintals per hectare is an average derived from very disparate figures. The average for Sardinia is below 10 quintals, dipping to 9 and even 8. If you take the figures for certain zones of Lombardy, instead, the average at times is above 30 quintals per hectare. Now, picture the conditions of the farmer who produces 8 quintals per hectare and those of the farmer who produces 30 and you will understand, if you reflect a bit, what fascism's policy in the countryside is.

Who is it that harvests 30 quintals of wheat per hectare from his fields? Thirty quintals of wheat per hectare are harvested above all by the big landowner, by the one who owns the most fertile land, has the biggest and most specialized equipment and has a large amount of capital to invest in the land, which permits him to use large quantities of chemical fertilizers, etc. It's clear that the unit cost of producing 30 quintals of wheat per hectare is much lower than the unit cost of producing only 8 quintals of wheat per hectare. This means that the import duty on wheat doesn't favor those who harvest 8 quintals per hectare, but those who harvest 30. Of course, this isn't true in the absolute sense. If it weren't for the import duty on wheat, those who harvest 8 quintals per hectare wouldn't even be able to plant wheat. They are generally small independent farmers who eat all the wheat they produce. The import duty on wheat does not affect them insofar as they do not produce for the market. The middle peasant, instead, who does produce for the market, usually is short of capital and must sell his wheat before it has ripened, while it is still in the field. He is obliged to sell it before the price is set. In this regard, we can see a characteristic feature of fascist policy. In some years, the import duty on wheat has been increased on the eve of the harvest, that is to say when the middle peasants have already sold their goods. We can see inequalities here. The wheat harvest is bought up in such a way as to favor the big capitalists, the usurers, the banks. And this is a reward the government gives to the large-scale wheat growers as compensation for the capital invested in their big farms.

The whole mechanism of the import duty on wheat and of the "wheat battle" is designed to favor farms with high productivity, those with high average crop yields. All the disadvantages fall on the small farmer who consumes all he produces, who has been forced to plant wheat where before he planted other crops because the price of these crops has slumped heavily as a result of the crisis. The big growers, the big farms, the agrarian capitalists and sometimes even the big tenant farmers and sharecroppers obtain enormous advantages instead.

But the "wheat battle" also increases the price of bread for the entire population. It therefore represents a tribute levied on all the workers, on the whole population, in favor of the big growers, in favor of the richest rural strata. The "wheat battle" corresponds to a process of differentiation in the countryside, a process that fascism found and accentuated, but that it also has instigated in part. What fundamental result is obtained in the countryside by means of the "wheat battle"? A larger investment of capital in agriculture. This means that, through a larger investment of capital, the battle brings about a strengthening in the countryside of the positions of capital, of the banks, of those who have money. Owing to the "wheat battle," the great trusts that manufacture chemical fertilizers, farm machinery, etc. have attained a formidable position. Montecatini, for example, controls 100 percent of the production of chemical fertilizers, which it sells at certain prices—prices that it keeps high thanks to its monopoly position. Finance capital, the banks are penetrating the countryside more and more. The "wheat battle" means the dominance of finance capital in the countryside.

Essentially, these are the chief results of the "wheat battle": the extension of production is due principally to larger investments of capital; the increase of output per hectare strengthens the big growers, the big farms, the big capitalists; and this increase, obtained thanks mainly to the import duty on wheat, reinforces the positions of the richest elements in the countryside, of the agrarian capitalists, of the banks, of finance capital.

Let's look at some other policy directives of fascism in the countryside: "comprehensive land reclamation." What is it? Here again we mustn't just laugh at what fascism says. Fascism made a grandiose plan requiring the investment of two billion lire a year to reclaim two million hectares of land. Fascism has not been able to realize this plan. In 1932-33 it was forced to cut back on its plan (mind you: its *plan*) by 9%; in 1933-34 the plan was scaled down by 36%; in 1934-35 it was scaled down by 56%; and, finally, for 1935-36 a 79% cutback is foreseen. I repeat, these cutbacks have been made on the plan; in the course of its implementation, the plan has undergone considerable additional curtailment.

You know what reclamation means. To reclaim land means taking land that today is swampland, not only non-arable but not even habitable, and making it produce; it means draining it of water and then cultivating it. In other words, two kinds of reclamation are necessary: hydraulic reclamation, which consists in clearing the underbrush, plowing the land and planting it.

What is needed to carry out these plans? (Again I repeat that we shouldn't make fun of what fascism does. What can we make fun of? The way fascism crows over the results of land reclamation. In effect, the results are scanty, very scanty. Not scanty, however, are the social results in the countryside, the shifts of classes and of class groupings that comprehensive land reclamation has brought about in the countryside.) "Comprehensive land reclamation" means an investment of capital in land, in agriculture. Enormous sums of capital are required for "hydraulic reclamation." Even larger amounts of capital are required for agricultural reclamation. On the basis of the state's decision, landowners are obliged to begin the work of reclamation. The state intervenes with certain forms of aid. Landowners must form consortiums. The large and medium-scale landowners join these consortiums. (The small landowners join them only in a few regions—for example, in Istria, Sardinia, etc.) What happens is that the small and medium-scale landowner cannot meet the expenses of the consortium year after year. Thus, in the consortiums the small landowner is expropriated and the medium-scale landowner runs into debt and tends to be expropriated. The groupings of large landowners strengthen their position in relation to the small and medium-scale landowners in the consortiums. These, then, are the most evident social results as of today. And they are not to be scorned.

Land reclamation has a decisive importance in Italy. Take a

fertile zone like Lombardy: it is all land that has been reclaimed and improved with an investment of capital down through the centuries. This investment is continuing today at a slower rate due to the crisis, but it is continuing. And it is being accompanied by social phenomena of extreme interest—phenomena that is leading to a greater class differentiation in the countryside, to a prospering of the rich and a pauperization of the poor.

But is there a difference between today's and yesterday's land reclamation? In certain areas no, in others yes! We mustn't forget that Italy had a very large current of emigration before the war. This current consisted essentially of peasants, of agricultural day laborers, who went to America to work and sent money back to Italy. The contribution to the agricultural improvement of a number of zones came through this, let's call it, "enrichment" of certain strata. But this was a feature of the prewar years. Today, the emigratory phenomenon has vanished. The tendency of agricultural workers to emigrate, with the formation of small and medium-sized landholdings by means of the earnings saved up by agricultural laborers and small peasants abroad, no longer can be noted as a characteristic social phenomenon.

What are the new landholdings? Let's see what measures fascism has taken for so-called domestic colonization. Starting in 1928, six thousand farm families were transplanted from one region to another. In 1933-34, the total number of such families came to two thousand. These families are settled in territories where, with drainage completed, the work of agricultural improvement is begun. This phenomenon is linked to a series of ties created between the families and the consortiums, for which these new so-called "landowners" are born under the star of indebtedness to the consortiums—a debt that grows bigger and bigger as the agricultural crisis grows worse. But this is not the characteristic rural phenomenon. The characteristic phenomenon is given by capitalist penetration and by a whole series of other modifications that fascism's policy has produced and that tend to reinforce the positions of the capitalists, of the biggest landowners and of finance capital. I am referring to the consortiums.

What are the consortiums? They are obligatory unions of the growers of a given product, unions whose scope is the setting of crop prices. In these consortiums, the small and medium-scale growers run up against the large grower; they find themselves at his mercy. The consortium is an instrument of the large growers for subjugating the small and medium-scale ones. Crop prices are set by the large growers. As we already have seen in the land-reclamation consortiums, in these consortiums there is a tendency to limit and expropriate the small and medium-scale landowners.

Then, to what we have said on fascism's policy in the countryside, we must add fiscal policy, which is designed particularly to hit the owner-operator. The owner-operator is taxed twice as much as the non-working landowner: he is taxed as a farm operator and as a laborer. You know how many taxes there are today, especially in the countryside. A tax is paid for having a cart, for slaughtering a pig, for having a dog, for owning a gun. These grinding taxes, especially heavy for the small and medium-scale growers, worsen their conditions.

What's the result? The result is that since 1927 there has been a tendency in the Italian countryside of the number of small and medium-scale growers to diminish and a tendency (I say tendency, and we must be careful not to look upon it as a *fait accompli)* of the small and medium-scale farms that sprang up in the postwar period to disappear. This tendency is stronger in mountain and hill zones than on the plains, but it exists everywhere. Again we can see how fascism's economic policy reinforces the positions of the strongest—of the agrarian capitalists, of the rich peasants, of finance capital.

Characteristic is the index offered us by the figures regarding the auctioning off of rural properties. These numbered 1,620 in 1927, came to 2,600 in 1929, rising to 3,400 in 1930, 4,000 in 1931, and reached 5,800 in 1932. We can see a roughly fourfold increase from 1927 to 1932. This trend can be seen throughout the Italian agricultural economy. Fascism says the opposite. Fascism says the trend is toward the disappearance of the landless farm worker and the creation of new strata of sharecroppers and small farmers.

Is this true? No, it's not true! Read Comrade Marabini's articles attentively and you will see a very ample documentation demonstrating how this is not true.[2]

Briefly, let's try to see what the fascist policy of "phasing out day labor in agriculture" means. Why is it said that a policy of "phasing out day labor in agriculture" is being implemented? Because groups of unemployed agricultural laborers are taken and installed on some of the richest peasants' worst tracts of land under forms of contracts which do not in the least transform the landless day laborer into a landowner. These contracts are just an instrument tying the agricultural laborer to a piece of land, land which must be cultivated under particular contractual terms. The terms of these contracts are a far sight worse than the terms of sharecropping contracts; they hark back to feudal relations. And let's see what piece of land is given to the agricultural day laborer: it's the poorest land that can be found in the zone. The laborer must do all the work of clearing for tillage, he's obliged to plant a given crop and to supply the agricultural tools, and he receives a share that is always less than half and sometimes even less than one-third of the harvest.

The share generally averages about one-third. The unemployed agricultural day laborers are thus forced to live on a given piece of land from dawn to dusk and, under most contracts, to make their whole families work it. Fascism no longer regards them as day laborers. These are servile economic forms that are being reintroduced into Italian agriculture by fascism. These servile economic forms are worsening rural class relations. Thus, we can see how the trend in the countryside is not at all to the formation of new strata of farmers, but rather to the creation of semi-proletarian strata that are even worse off than the landless farm laborers inasmuch as they have lost the characteristics of the farm laborer without having acquired those of the farm owner.

The fascist dictatorship talks a good deal about "phasing out day labor in agriculture." And this does have a moderate influence. Not everyone understands what this policy of phasing out day labor in agriculture is, what it means. Many believe the demagogy of fascism. In certain rural zones even some comrades are influenced by it. We had to talk for hours even with a Party official who told us: "After all, at least my father has something to eat now. That means there's been an improvement." We had to go deep into this problem to show him what this "improvement" really was.

Now, on the whole, what are the results of fascist policy in the countryside? The situation today is completely different from the one that existed in the immediate postwar years. Two things were always said in Italy: that, on the one hand, there were very large remnants of the feudal economy in the Italian countryisde; and, on the other, that a situation existed for which the fundamental thrust was aimed at acquiring land, a situation for which elements of the bourgeois-democratic revolutionary movement were to be found in the countryside. (The proletarian revolution will have to solve the problem of giving land to the peasants since this is the need, the fundamental aspiration, of the Italian peasantry.)

Has fascism changed something? Yes, it has changed something in that it has made the positions of industry much more solid, much stronger that those of agriculture in Italy; it has strengthened the positions of the banks throughout the country; it has strengthened the positions of finance capital throughout the economy. Does this mean, perhaps, that the remnants of feudalism have disappeared? This is something our Party has not yet looked into. For example, our Party has not yet made a study of the remnants of feudalism in Sicily, where they are notoriously stronger than they are elsewhere. But we can say that where these feudal remnants do exist, fascism has not destroyed them because it is precisely on this stratum that fascism leans for support in Sicily, for example. The great estate owners, the barons, represent a stratum closely tied to fascism. But does this mean there has been no development of finance capital in Sicily? Banco di Sicilia has experienced enormous growth as a rural bank. But to whom are its loans made? They are made to the great estate owners. Therefore, we are not in the presence of a penetration of capital in the countryside that is breaking up the latifundia, but rather of a penetration of capital through the feudal elements, a penetration that is strengthening the position of these elements.

Fascism's struggle against the mafia was essentially a struggle against the stratum of landowners which had been forming and which, while coming out against the revolutionary movement, nonetheless was eroding the latifundia. You know what the mafia is and that it is a complex phenomenon. Coming between the barons and the peasants of Sicily there is a whole stratum of intermediaries formed by the large tenant farmers, tenants, subtenants. There is a whole series of gradations between the owner and the worker. This is where the mafia arises. Each of these groups forms a clique which on the one hand fights against the feudal lord and on the other endeavors to keep the peasant down. Fascism has intervened not to shift the class positions, but to buttress the positions of the great estate owners. So much for Sicily.

As for the other regions, the general phenomenon is represented by a larger use of capital, of machinery, of chemical fertilizers. We have already seen that a larger per-hectare yield of wheat means a larger capital investment. Is the land problem posed differently today as a consequence? This is a political problem that needs to be answered.

The great masses of farm workers are landless; they are agricultural wage laborers, in large part permanently or almost permanently unemployed, reduced to the status of semi-proletarians. What do they want? Might they perhaps be inclined to solve the land problem differently than before? Do objective conditions exist for posing the land problem from the standpoint of a reform? No, these objective conditions do not exist. Today, there no longer is a tendency of the poor strata to grow wealthy, but there is an opposite trend—a trend toward their definitive ruin.

On the other hand, has the drive to acquire land changed character? No! The mass strata of farm workers want land; they want to become landowners through revolution. Not agrarian reform, therefore, but agrarian revolution: this is how the problem is posed.

Fascism has preserved the feudal remnants; it has extended the application of sharecropping contracts, which are one of the most characteristic expressions of these remnants; it has strengthened the positions of finance capital and all of capitalism's positions in the countryside; but it has not created a tendency to solve the land problem through reform and, on the contrary, has reinforced the tendency to solve the land problem through revolution.

The overall results of fascism's policy in the countryside have led to a narrowing of fascism's original bases. What are fascism's bases today? They are plainly capitalistic. In the countryside, they are represented by the big farmers, the big landowners. Strata of wealthy peasants also are tied to fascism, but strong discontent is growing even among them under the pressure of the crisis.

For the great mass of the rural working population, the land problem is more acute than it was before. The objective conditions for an alliance between the proletariat and the mass of agricultural workers are more favorable today than in the past. This does not mean, however, that this alliance can come about on its own, automatically. The objective conditions are much easier, but the subjective conditions are much harder. The strengthening of capitalism in the countryside has made revolutionary work much more difficult. The forms of control, which previously were much weaker in the countryside than in the cities, have been reinforced considerably.

This sets us vast and difficult immediate tasks; this means that our Party's agrarian program, our agitation and our work in the countryside have acquired far greater importance today than in the past.

appendix

Where is the Force of Italian Fascism?[1]

THE PROBLEM of Italian fascism is still arousing deep interest in the international arena, but not in the same way as in the past, when fascism was a new development and the interest consisted in seeking *the essence of fascism*. Today, there no longer are any disagreements among us in this regard. The definition of fascism as given by the Communist International in its congresses, and in an even more precise manner by the 13th Plenary Meeting of the Executive Committee of the Communist International, not only is completely correct, not only is the result of a study conducted for years by the Communist International, but by now is recognized as exact by important strata of workers, petty bourgeois and intellectuals that are not yet under the direct influence of the Communist parties. In a word, the conception that fascism is the open form of the dictatorship of the most reactionary groups of the bourgeoisie under present-day historical conditions is now a largely popular conception. *But how* does fascism succeed in maintaining and defending capitalism's power over the working class and the great working masses today, under the increasingly grave conditions—be it a question of the economic or of the political situation— which the bourgeoisie is forced to deal with?

This problem, naturally, is not new. Each and every one of us knows enough to repeat that fascism defends and maintains the bourgeoisie's power by means of open violence and terror, prosecuting a ruthless offensive against the workers' conditions of existence, destroying every possibility of the workers' movement and of the great masses to organize autonomously, muzzling public opinion, etc. Each and every one of us is able to repeat these things. But for all that they are correct, do they thoroughly explain the reality of things? And then, when we examine the way to combat fascism, can we content ourselves with affirmations of a general kind, or mustn't we delve into a much more concrete analysis of fascist policy instead?

Let's take the example of Italy. Fascism has been in power for twelve years there. From the very moment it took power, it immediately ran up against a series of grave political difficulties, but for a few years the economic conditions remained relatively favorable for it (the period of relative stabilization). Since then, the economic situation has grown worse, slowly at first, then at an exceedingly fast pace. The world crisis has found in the Italian economy a body already weakened by grave illnesses (the financial crisis of 1926-27 and its consequences, the acute agrarian crisis, etc.) and has jolted it hard, exacerbating a whole series of very serious contradictions. Nonetheless, fascism has held up. Since 1927, wages have undergone an average real reduction of over fifty percent. The phenomenon of *permanent* unemployment has reappeared in the Italian economy, affecting hundreds of thousands of people. But whereas in the past, before the war, this phenomenon was confined to the countryside at the very most and its consequences were attenuated by a strong and constant current of emigration, today unemployment is spread to the cities and to the industrial proletariat, and the migratory currents no longer exist except at a paltry level. The condition of life of the working masses, particularly in a number of agricultural regions, has been reduced to an extremely, incredibly low level that cannot be compared to the level of sixty years ago, right after the formation of the unified nation-state. Back then, the bourgeoisie itself seemed shocked by the miserable situation of the masses and some of its statesmen denounced that situation in investigative studies that still are famous. The conditions to which the masses have been relegated and the country's economic situation in general are such that a comparison between the present situation and what fascism promised twelve years ago in its initial program would seem paradoxical today.

But fascism is holding up. What are the bases of its resistance? It seems to me that this problem is of particular interest when speaking of Italian fascism. A systematic discussion of this problem cannot but be extremely instructive both for us Italian Communists—since by discussing it we are led inevitably, given our experience, to discover the numerous and serious errors we have committed—and for our comrades from other countries, who certainly can learn many things from our experience.

And I ask my readers to excuse me if I feel obliged to repeat once again that, in studying the development and the policy of fascism in the various countries, one must be careful not to mechanically transpose the experiences of the development of Italian fascism to other countries. I would also like to add that not only when the nature of fascism is discussed, but the *concrete forms* of its policy also are considered in detail, the danger of falling into clichés and meaningless statements grows appreciably; therefore, it's more necessary than ever to steer clear of false analogies. I believe it useful for the comrades from the other countries of fascist dictatorship and the comrades of the Bolshevik Communist Party, who have the experience of the illegal struggle against the czarist autocracy, to examine the facts we are speaking of, confront them with their own experience, and help us deepen the study of our problems and find what in our experience can be generalized and applied to other countries.

The Fascist Party, a New Type of Bourgeois Party

The first point I would like to dwell on is this: what fascism has been able to accomplish in the field of the political organization of the bourgeoisie thanks to the objective circumstances and numerous other elements, among which the weakness of the revolutionary movement is not the least important. The Italian bourgeoisie did not possess a strong political organization before the advent of fascism. This is an indisputable fact. There were a great number of parties in Italy, but they mainly had an electoral and local character, without well-defined programs, and from the standpoint of organization and cadres they were unsubstantial. The bourgeois statesmen, and particularly Giovanni Giolitti, who was the right-hand man of the industrial bourgeoisie, of the banks and of the monarchy before and even after the war, were always anxious not to create strong bourgeois parties equipped with a well-defined program and solidly organized, but on the contrary to impede the formation of such parties. Their art of government consisted, rather, in breaking up the existing parties and forming a parliamentary majority through compromises, corruption, maneuvers, etc.

Thus, when two big, solid, well-organized and disciplined mass political parties—the Socialist Party and the Popular (Catholic) Party—appeared right after the war and powerfully asserted themselves in the country's political life, the Italian bourgeoisie's whole system of government was thrown out of kilter.

All in all, the Italian bourgeoisie had but one unified organization: the Freemasonry. But the Freemasonry's ideology no longer suited the struggle that the bourgeoisie had undertaken for the purpose of organizing its *open* dictatorship. This is why at a certain point fascism concentrated its blows against the Freemasonry.

Fascism not only set itself the task of creating a solid, united political organization of the bourgeoisie, but it has also succeeded in accomplishing this task. Fascism has given the Italian bourgeoisie what it always lacked, namely, a strong, centralized, disciplined, *single* party equipped with its own armed force.

One might object that the Fascist Party is not a party in the true sense of the word, in the traditional sense of the word, because its structure and workings are not democratic, because regular discussions do not take place inside it, because there is no form of election of officials at the rank-and-file level, etc. All this is true, but these objections only serve to demonstrate that the Fascist Party is a bourgeois party of a special type; it is a "new type" of party of the bourgeoisie, adapted to the conditions stemming from the period of the breakup of capitalism and the period of proletarian revolution, adapted above all to the conditions of the bourgeoisie's open dictatorship over the proletariat and the great working masses.

The bourgeoisie is tending today to create parties of this type in every country. The presence of a bourgeois party of this type constitutes one of the characteristic aspects of the organization of the fascist dictatorship.

To be sure, the creation of this new kind of party does not come about without difficulties; generally, it is a complex process full of contradictions, full of twists and turns. In this regard, I would like to point out that various times during the first years of the fascist dictatorship we expressed a unilateral judgment on this process; we focused our attention solely on the resistance that the old bourgeois political formations were putting up to the march of fascism; we felt, back then, that each of these instances of resistance ought to have developed immediately to the point of creating the conditions for an insuperable "political crisis"; and we forgot, in effect, that the decisive element capable of reducing fascism's advantage can only be the anti-fascist struggle of the masses. This error of evaluation, which gives rise to inexact projections on the development of the situation, was committed likewise in other countries and is still being repeated even today.

Obviously, it's not true—and to affirm it would also be a grave theoretical error—that the creation of a new "type" of party of the bourgeoisie suppresses the antagonisms within capitalism's ruling classes. On the contrary, it is necessary to emphasize that the creation of this new type of party corresponds to a deepening of these contradictions. Nevertheless, seeing that the conflicts do not come out into the open except when they've become very profound, the bourgeois ruling classes are able to present themselves *to the masses* as a unified and coherent force.

Let's take the Italian working masses as an example. For eight years, they've been reduced to reading nothing but the fascist press when they can't get their hands on the Communist Party's underground press. And the fascist press tries first and foremost to hide the disagreements agitating the ruling classes and to present the forces of the bourgeoisie as united, compact, in the ranks of fascism. This is one of the prime factors of the spread of fascist influence among the masses. It is a factor of the highest psychological importance. Its effect cannot be restricted if we are unable, by ensuring a wide circulation of the illegal press, to largely discredit fascism in the eyes of the masses, to contrast its words to its deeds, to show the true spirit of its campaigns, etc. But only the movement of the masses can result in the destruction of fascism. Every time a mass movement, however limited, explodes, hesitations in the ranks of fascism can be observed at once; and when the movements multiply and spread, the hesitations end up by giving rise to doubt as to the validity of fascism's official policy line. And so "crises" of the fascist organization are produced on the local scale and, at times, even on the national scale, as we saw recently when Arpinati, Mussolini's former Minister of the Interior, was arrested along with 200 other leading Fascists because he was for a change in fascist policy toward social democracy.*

All this clearly shows how dangerous is the belief that fascism is bound to collapse by itself as a result of the spontaneous explosion of the internal contradictions undermining its regime. This belief was spread widely in Italy by social democracy and the old democratic leaders, and also filtered into the ranks of our Party. Hence the opportunistic tendencies "to wait for" a change in the situation before doing something. Hence, too, the impulse that led the Party to turn inward on itself, to lose the exact conception of its own functions and of the

* In order to avert such crises, fascism pays the utmost attention to its cadres and renews them frequently. The most important operation of this kind was carried out when fascism set about organizing the "totalitarian" state.

On that occasion, Mussolini rigorously applied the directive that *fascism cannot organize the state with the same cadres that had helped it seize power.* All the old squad leaders, of petty-bourgeois origins but declassed, the old officers, etc. saw their place of leadership in the Fascist Party's local organizations taken away from them, and a good part of them took refuge in the boards of directors of the big companies, of the insurance companies, etc., where they have grown rich and become completely bourgeois without disturbing anyone. In that period, the local leadership posts were entrusted to direct representatives of the industrial and agrarian bourgeoisie. But later, in periods in which the mass movement became dangerous, Mussolini turned again to the old cadres, and they were the ones who saved him during the Matteotti crisis by forcing him to take an intransigent line.—*Author.*

functions of the working class in the fight against the fascist dictatorship, to give up everyday mass organizing and thus cut itself off from the masses.

It is a grave theoretical and political error to think that the setting up of the fascist dictatorship suppresses the contradictions among the various groups of the bourgeoisie. But it would be a much graver error to think that by founding a unified party of the bourgeoisie, by creating a fascist organization that embraces the majority of the population and all the forms of its life, fascism can ultimately suppress the fundamental antagonism that exists between the class content of the fascist dictatorship and the interests and aspirations of the working class and of the great laboring masses which it is trying to mislead and subjugate. On the contrary, sheltered by this would-be "totalitarian" and monolithic system, capitalist exploitation is increasing considerably, creating the objective conditions for an extreme sharpening of the class struggle—a struggle that can be contained only for a certain period of time, exploding in the end with all the more force and impetus. From this point of view, nothing concrete or real corresponds to the fundamental slogan with which fascism has been operating for a number of years: that of the "corporative state," of the state in which class contradictions and differences allegedly have been suppressed. In its first years in power, fascism was able to give the impression that its policy was favoring overall economic development. It was, in reality, a quesion of an outgrowth of the period of relative stabilization, when, after having gained victory in the world war and over revolutionary working-class movement, Italian imperialism, the "paupers' " imperialism, was able to buttress itself a little by raising production. Fascism contributed to this expansion by wiping out the revolutionary organizations and heaping favors on the capitalists and bankers. However, the objective economic contradictions had been sharpened quite rapidly by the very growth of production, the situation changed, and the difficulties kept piling up until the economic crisis broke out. In parallel, the class contradictions sharpened, and at an even faster pace than the economic crisis. Fascism's changeover to the "totalitarian system" (which replaced the system of compromises with other political groups), the complete suppression of parliamentarianism, the stepping up of repression, the exceptional laws (this "exception" has been with us for eight years!) and, finally, the efforts to drive the masses into the fascist organization, were fascism's response to this sharpening of the class antagonisms.

This response, however, did not solve the problem by any means. Despite its unceasing efforts, fascism finds it impossible to build a corporative state "above the classes" and, precisely for this, to eliminate the class struggle. The class struggle of the workers and of the great masses always grows anew, in new conditions, under new forms, with new prospects. Nothing better demonstrates the futility of the task fascism has set itself—to create a state "above the classes"—than the variety and instability of the forms of the fascist organization: the fact that fascism is forced continuously to change its organizational methods and forms in order to meet the danger that the objective situation and the masses' will to struggle represent for it.

The objective contradictions that the fascist regime cannot overcome offer possibilities of struggle which our Party ought to have utilized much more largely in the past, and which it must utilize very extensively in the current situation.

The Working Class, Terror and Fascist Organizing of the Masses

The Italian bourgeoisie had succeeded in creating groups of labor aristocracy and corrupting a part of the "leaders" of the working-class movement. Ever since fascism seized power, and especially since the economic difficulties began to be felt, since the agrarian crisis in the countryside grew worse and the country's whole economy found itself wallowing in the crisis—since then, profound changes have come about in this field. It would be wrong, however, to assume that fascism has reduced all the categories of factory workers, all the groups of laborers, to the selfsame level. Differences persist, and they are not negligible.

The most energetic leveling action is being carried out in the countryside. A difference still persists, for example, between the average wage of the agricultural day laborers in the South and in the Po Valley; wages are lower and misery is greater in the South. But before the advent of fascism, there were important groups of agricultural day laborers in the Po Valley who, on the whole, could have been regarded as privileged because by struggling and organizing they had reached the point of assuring themselves a greater number of work-days each year. It can be said that these groups have vanished today; and this, I think, best explains the fact that most of the mass movements take place in the countryside and among the agricultural day laborers in particular.

If we take the industrial working class, we'll see things are different. There are still some categories of workers—the printers, for example—that have preserved their character as "privileged" trades compared to others. The printers' wages have been cut too, but they are still above average. Furthermore, the fascist union belonging to this corporation does not differ from the printers' old reformist organization. It is substantially the same organization as before, but with the twist that the Fascists installed themselves in it without the reformist leaders having offered any mass resistance. In reality, they became its bosses with the aid and abetment of the reformist leaders. Today, this organization functions as it functioned before, and in the past years, if I am not mistaken, there have been only two movements of an economic nature among the printers. The same thing goes for a number of other trades—the hatters, for example, whose reformist organization also had a strongly pronounced corporative character. As for the seamen, there was a rather long period of time in which the organization's old officials collaborated with the Fascists, which enabled the latter to take over the whole organization and consolidate their hold on the mass.

On the other hand, if we examine the fundamental categories of the industrial proletariat (metallurgy, textiles, chemicals, construction, etc.), we see that fascism completely destroyed the old legal class organization without leaving a trace of it; that it destroyed it equally well as a trade-union organization in the proper sense of the term and as a factory organization (shop stewards). The fascist union organization in these corporations has nothing in common with the old organization. Even the type of labor contract is different. But one mustn't believe that conditions are identical in all the corporations. The metalworkers' wages (that is, the wages set by the fascist labor contracts) are a little higher than those in other trades, and among the metalworkers' themselves one can also note that in some regions (in Turin, for example, which is the country's most important metallurgy center) they are in turn slightly higher than elsewhere.

The situation in the factories is somewhat more complicated because the fascist labor contract is never applied generally and uniformly to all workers. The bosses set up big wage differentials from worker to worker, and the least favored workers are obliged to accept these differentials without protesting, for fear of being fired and left jobless.

It must be said that, in general, the number of workers belonging to the *skilled* categories has been drastically reduced. The work force is made up mainly of "semi-skilled workers," employed particularly in mass production, and unskilled workers. The percentage of women employed in industry has risen, while the workers' store of skills has generally diminished. From this viewpoint, there really has been a leveling. But at the same time we are witnessing a new phenomenon: small groups of workers, ideologically and organically tied to fascism much more closely than the other workers, have formed in the factories and now constitute a special "aristocracy" from the political standpoint. All these elements do not come from the ranks of the more skilled workers, nor are they "foremen"; but they nonetheless constitute fascism's point of support in the factories, and the bosses are trying hard to maintain this point of support. In judging the forces that fascism can count on in a shop, one has to gauge not the number of workers who are members of the Fascist Party (because membership is semi-obligatory and sometimes comes automatically with the job), but the number of workers politically and organically tied more closely to fascism.

I have insisted on these facts because, in my opinion, they show very well how the *problem of terror* under Italian fascism's twelve-year dictatorship must be posed. The various points of support that fascism has been able to gain among the masses have served it and are still serving it to sustain and develop its organizing of the populace. In the fascist dictatorship's relations with working masses, the important, characteristic aspect is precisely the combining of the methods of open violence and terror with the methods of the more or less forced marshalling of the masses into an organization created by the Fascists. Open violence and terror are used against the Communist Party constantly, unreservedly, fully, brutally, to shatter its cadres and its ties with the masses, to make its work impossible. With regard to the cadres of the social-democratic parties (disbanded and outlawed like ours), the situation changes: terror is not used against them in the same way as it is against us, and it rapidly gives ways to attempts of corruption, to offers of positions in the fascist hierarchy and so forth. As for the masses, fascism's policy consists in making terror a continual threat, although it is not always employed against them in an identical and massive way. In Florence, for example, the most noted "subversive" elements (Communists for the most part) are dragged down to regional Fascist headquarters every so often and beaten up for no plausible motive. But the local Fascist club for that sector simultaneously conducts a pseudo-"popular" action among the masses. If a husband beats his wife and she goes to the Fascist club to complain, the local officials take her defense, summon the husband, warn him and order him to put an end to such mistreatment. Also, the club officials might intervene in favor of a tenant threatened with eviction by his landlord, or maybe even lend aid in money to a family in need. In that very same city, *all* those who cast a negative vote on the occasion of the last plebiscite were taken to Fascist headquarters and beaten with untold barbarity.

But the most common form of terror is what could be called "economic" terror. Every worker knows not only that he can't find work if he's not a member of a fascist organization, but that he'll lose his job if he even covertly demonstrates his anti-fascist feelings, if he doesn't take part in fascist demonstrations, if he's suspected of being an active anti-fascist.

Furthermore, an extreme violence is used against the masses every time their movements spread and deepen, whenever the local Fascist officials realize that neither promises nor small concessions would serve to quell the ferment.

Combining all these methods, fascism is able to regiment all the working masses into one or more fascist organizations and to establish a manifold, refined system of control at every moment even on the workers; a system that is very difficult to evade and that makes it possible to penetrate the workers ranks' with fascist ideology in the most diverse forms.

It is evident that the struggle against a regime that establishes its ties with the masses in this way cannot develop if it is not routed through the penetration of the enemy organization's ranks; if the Communist vanguard—relying heavily on its underground organization and on the class unions, never hiding the Party's true face and constantly carrying on agitation and the fight for the final goal, for the revolutionary overthrow of the fascist dictatorship—does not succeed in transferring the center of the *Communist vanguard's mass work to that organization*. It is evident, however, that the attitude fascism has had to take toward the masses, and the efforts through which it tries to regiment and influence them, cannot but create manifold possibilities of engaging in legal and semi-legal work to mobilize the masses against fascism itself.

Fascism's Maneuvers and Its Different Forms of Organization

The affirmation that fascism's organizations cover nearly all of the country's population is confirmed by statistics.* But I would not want

* According to the latest statistics, the fascist organizations have twelve million members, distributed as follows:

Fascist Party	1,096,000
Fascist Youth	336,000
Balilla and Young Italians (youngsters up to age 15)	3,659,000
University Groups	53,000
Fascist Teachers' Association	83,000
Fascist Civil Servants' Association	110,000
Association of Workers of State Industry	32,000
Fascist Railwaymen's Association	99,000
Postal-Workers' Association	48,000
Fascist Trade Unions (including 1,659,000 industrial workers)	4,042,000
Dopolavoro	2,000,000
Mutual-Aid Associations	1,200,000

this affirmation to give comrades the impression that the fascist regime is something solid, compact, like a wall against which it is useless to beat one's head. On the contrary, there is a profound, immeasurable contradiction between the fascist dictatorship and the masses of workers that it regiments in its organizations. We are dealing with a class antagonism that is growing objectively worse under the weight of the economic difficulties and of fascist policy—a policy whose plundering character is being accentuated to the benefit of the most reactionary groups of the bourgeoisie. And this contradiction manifests itself clearly inside of the fascist organizational structure, causing great instability in its forms.

The type of fascist trade-union organization varies a good deal from trade to trade (and we have already seen the reasons for this). But it also varies from region to region and from moment to moment. In Turin and Milan, the fascist trade-union officials try to tie the workers to the organization, ask them to frequent union headquarters, compel them to attend union meetings, and hold these meetings during working hours in the factory yards, closing the exit gates. In Apulia (southern Italy), where the misery of the masses is much greater than it is elsewhere, and where a strong tendency to violent and spontaneous mass movements reigns, the fascist unions almost never organize meetings; and at the doors of union headquarters stand two guards who don't let the farm workers in except one at a time, for a short talk, and prevent any assembly in front of the doors. In La Spezia (an important industrial center), despite a certain number of errors and hesitations, our organization was able in 1933 to capitalize on numerous union meetings the Fascists called, as a means of exhorting the masses to struggle and strike. It was therefore decided on orders from higher up that the trade unions should not hold any more meetings. Meetings were not resumed until after our organization had been destroyed by the work of a spy. The saddest thing is that we were organized in such a way that the spy was able to bring all our mass work to a halt just by demolishing the center of the Party's clandestine apparatus.

In general, the fascist unions' form of organization has changed repeatedly since 1927. Originally, the organization was set up on a trade basis and there was a central federative body that directed all the categories. The upshot was that during the first congress this body held, the discontent of the masses was spoken for by the Fascist officials themselves, who were feeling the pressure of the workers. And they did this so well that a scandal ensued. The central body was suppressed, only the trade organizations were left standing, and an attempt was made to fall back on the local unions by linking them to the factories through a network of shop stewards. But things grew even worse: the industrialists demanded the suppression of the shop stewards, the locals were eliminated as well and were replaced by province-wide structures. This system, which accentuated the organization's bureaucratic nature,was abandoned in turn when it was discovered that it was making the Fascist officials lose direct contact with the masses.

It is not my intention to enumerate all the transformations the fascist trade-union organization has undergone. I only want to underscore the importance of these transformations since they demonstrate that,despite everything, fascism has not succeeded and cannot succeed in solidly winning the masses over, and is forced continually to struggle, to maneuver, to adapt itself in every way in order to stay in contact with them, prevent their movement, control them as best it can.

A good understanding of all these facts also enables us to put the problem of working inside the fascist organization in its true light and to defeat the opinion of those who, when this work is discussed, only know how to draw attention to the "dangers" it holds, as if the fascist mass organization were something coherent, compact, capable of absorbing and assimilating anyone who carries out class activity within it. This organization is, on the contrary, an amalgam of variable relations, a terrain on which struggle between fascism and the masses is constant, even though it does not always surface openly.

Fascism's capacity to modify its positions (while maintaining the fundamental class character of its dictatorship intact) in order to deal with new and more difficult situations becomes evident when one considers the different demagogic campaigns conducted by the Fascists in the course of recent years. The most interesting thing to observe is that since 1930 (i.e. following the outbreak of the worldwide crisis) Italian fascism has incredibly tightened its economic pressure on the masses, putting the slogan of "going to the masses" at the center of all its propaganda. What does this mean? It means that fascism, feeling its situation grow worse, has launched an all-out fight to maintain its influence on the working masses and extend it as much as possible, and to keep the objective difficulties from wrecking its organizational system. It can be said that fascism has made a fresh effort to renew its demagogy, to change the tone of its mass propaganda, every six months since 1930. For some time, all the propaganda has been concentrated on "corporativism," viewed as a system distinct from both capitalism and socialism. But even today, after Mussolini's latest speech confessing the dictatorship's *economic* "failure," the Fascist officials are making different proposals from the ones they were making six months ago during the plebiscite campaign. Back then, they were saying that corporativism had enabled Italy to feel the blows of the crisis less strongly than the other countries; today, they no longer are denying the gravity of the country's economic situation, but are babbling on about the possibility corporativism offers for dividing the sacrifices equally among all the classes, and are portraying war as inevitable and as a way out of the actual difficulties.

This capacity to maneuver with the aid of slogans and by modifying the organizational forms constitutes one of the most important factors of the "force" of Italian fascism. And this factor cannot be neutralized or eliminated except by intelligent, bold, tenacious and far-reaching action by the Party.

Thus, we have come now to the real heart of the problem, namely, the question of our policy and action.

The Movement of the Masses and the Communist Party's Remissness

In his speech to the Fourth Congress of the Communist International, Lenin, discussing the resolution of the Third Congress on the structure of the Communist Parties and on the methods and content of their work, dealt with the need for the foreign comrades to "study" the experience of Bolshevism and digest a piece of Russian experience. Addressing himself directly to the Italian comrades, who had just seen fascism come to power, he said: "Perhaps the Fascists in Italy, for example, will render us a great service by explaining to the Italians that they are not yet sufficiently enlightened and that their country is yet to be insured against the Black Hundreds."[2]

Our Party did not pay sufficient attention to these words, the last ones Comrade Lenin addressed to us and which express quite concisely the idea that only broad mass work, the consistent struggle of the Party and the coordination of its illegal work with its legal work can keep the fascist bands in check and impede, in particular, the penetration of fascist influence in several strata of workers. If we consider not only our Party's analyses of the situation and its general policy positions, but also its day-to-day political and organizational work (and the two things can never be examined separately), we must note in its activity as a whole a great delay in posing the problems of the struggle against fascism and in solving them in practice.

In our favor, we have the justification that ours was the first Party of the International that had to combat a fascist dictatorship, and that we did not always get that much help from those with more experience than us. We fought hard and courageously, and the masses never lost sight of us; but one cannot deny the fact that we were very slow to comprehend the forms in which the anti-fascist fight had to be waged so as to be effective and capable of countering the dictatorship's plans.

In 1927 and 1928, deep-going discussions developed at the center of our Party on the following problem: does the establishment of fascist dictatorship in a totalitarian form mean that no other regime but the dictatorship of the proletariat can succeed fascism, or do other historical and political prospects exist instead? Interesting discussions. But while we were engaged in them, fascism was laying the foundations of its mass organization, and our Party organizations, under the blows of reaction, were beginning to dry up, to turn inward on themselves, to content themselves with an exclusively internal and sectarian life, to cut themselves off from the masses. While we affirmed the *historical* inevitability of the proletarian revolution, we forgot that the essential thing is to create the *political* and *organic* conditions under which the working class can victoriously develop its revolutionary struggle. Our press carried interesting appraisals of the question of the fascist shop stewards—a question debated sharply by the fascist trade-union apparatus and the industrialists in 1927—28—but these assessments only appeared three months after the matter had been settled by order of Mussolini. And when the same question came up again in 1931 as a point of fascism's new mass policy, we limited ourselves to discussing the eventual "dangers" inherent in utilizing even part of the shop stewards for the purpose of broadening our legal activity and setting a company's workers in motion. And only today, in 1934, have we suddenly realized that wherever our comrades strive to set off rank-and-file movements and strikes in the factories, they are inevitably led to make use of part of the fascist shop stewards.

The examples could be increased. It seems to me that the essential is this: our Party did not understand fully and in time that the setting up of a totalitarian fascist dictatorship makes it imperative that the Communist vanguard not narrow the scope of its political action and of its "maneuvers," but that it extend it; that it "politick" courageously, giving the enemy no truce, pursuing him relentlessly and combating him on all grounds. And even when this necessity was understood, we did not know how to take swift advantage of all its implications.

Our Party's remissness therefore was and is *essentially political*. In a certain period (in 1927), we confined ourselves to mass leafletting and circulating newspapers, and we thought that the great number of these was sufficient to make up for everything. At other times (in 1929 and, later, in 1933), we had to work hard to reknit the Party's ties, since our mode of working had burned up our forces,and our cadres in the first place, too quickly. However, the key to all the mistakes we made both in the political and in the organizational field must be found in the fact that we lacked ability in transforming all the methods of our work rapidly and radically so as not to lose contact with any of the popular strata that fascism tries to influence and hold in a thousand ways. Only in 1931 did the Party's central leadership begin to pose the problems of this transformation; and the struggle to solve them did not begin to develop effectively until mid-1932, due also to the resistance that was encountered at the center itself.

The consequences of this political remissness of the Party are felt mainly in the following three fields: the way in which mass movements develop, the manner in which the phenomena of fascism's internal "crises" present themselves and the sharpness with which the youth question is raised for us.

Although their compass has been limited, a considerable number of mass movements, protest actions, street demonstrations and even strikes have taken place in Italy since 1930. We intend to carefully analyze the character of these movements and the Party's role in them in a forthcoming article. For the moment, we will limit ourselves to underscoring the characteristic and fundamental elements: the brevity of the demonstrations, the extreme difficulties the masses encounter in giving them larger dimensions, the ease with which the movement can be cut off and smothered by a fascist maneuver or through some partial economic concessions. Unless we are mistaken, the mass movements in Germany also have a similar character today. And in our view, based on a good many years of experience, this character will not disappear until the Communist vanguard establishes extremely solid and broad political and organic ties with the masses. But to reach this scope,it's not enough to leaflet and agitate. In a situation like ours, it's indispensable to penetrate all the fascist mass formations organically and broadly; it's indispensable that these organizations become the chief field of our mass work. It may seem paradoxical, but the following happened: the belief spread in our ranks (just as fascism was succeeding in harnessing the masses in its organizations and, in part, also in influencing them ideologically) that it would be enough for the Party to launch a *general* call to struggle and all the workers would rise up against the fascist dictatorship, their movements growing spontaneously and arriving at the general strike and insurrection. This opportunistic conception, a typical manifestation of the doctrine of spontaneity, hurt us greatly because it kept us from seeing the breadth of the political and organizational tasks which are incumbent on the Communist Party if it wants to drive the mass movement forward against the fascist dictatorship.

The matter is even more obvious when we come to the phenomena of "crises" in fascism. There have been phenomena of this kind in our country, too. There are many Fascists who circulate our press and read it willingly. There also are a good many cases of Fascists protesting, demonstrating and striking together with our comrades. I recall that one of our organizations held one of its conferences under the protection of a strong group of armed Fascists. But what happens afterward? What happens to all these individuals and groups influenced or even fully won over by us? Have we been able to bring all these groups and isolated individuals together so as to make their movement give birth to an open crisis of the fascist regime or of some of its important structures?

No, we still have not been able to do this. And the reason is that we have always leaned toward the small-scale work of "gnawing away" at the fascist organization on an individual basis, and not toward large-scale political work designed to create inside of it vast opposition currents capable of acting as a center of liaison among the numerous individuals who are not yet Communists or sympathizers, but who are dissatisfied and unhappy and can be led to fight against the existing order.

The German comrades especially must focus their attention on this problem. Hitler's storm troops include more workers and conceal more discontent than the Fascist Militia ever did; the circumstances are very favorable. However, I feel that the Facist chiefs' maneuvers undoubtedly will always have a chance of impeding the explosion of the general crisis of Hitler's regime until the Communist Party, through energetic political and organizational measures, succeeds in taking over the direction of this discontent and in channeling it towards precise political objectives.

In conclusion, one must not believe that the masses —regimented, organized and influenced by the Fascists—one fine day will move away from fascism spontaneously, as a matter of course, and come over to us, to the proletarian revolution. We must seek these masses out and *organize* their changeover to our side.

As far as young people are concerned, the problem is beginning to assume quite a grave aspect, and this gravity is coming to light elsewhere as well. The Party's isolation from the masses is particularly notable in the case of young people, to whom fascism devotes very special attention and who as yet have but little experience in the class struggle. The most alarming fact is that in certain cases a gap can be seen not only between the Party and young people, but even between the latter and the old working-class cadres who have the experience of the past struggle and never have submitted to fascism. Might this gap be due to the fact that the masses of young people are not discontent and militant? Absolutely not. Young workers are protesting against the conditions which fascism forces on them, and often with more violence than adult workers. But *all* the youth are regimented in the fascist organizations, while adults often feel a "moral" repugnance at joining these organizations in order to seek out the young, tie up with them, communicate to them the experience of the past struggle and direct them in today's struggle. Thus, young find themselves somehow "abandoned" to fascism, which does not neglect work or maneuvers or parades or sports propaganda or anything that can serve to bind itself to the young masses.

To conclude, we say that fascism carries out differentiated, manifold action among the masses, tailored to fit each moment and each category, each factory and each group and each particular stratum; and that this action still is not being combated effectively because the Party so far has not become adept, prompt, courageous and tenacious enough in its work among the masses to be able to break the links of the fascist organization and policy one by one and open the path to mass revolt. This, I feel, is the principal root of Italian fascism's resistance and force today.

Perhaps I ought to set forth here concretely and in detail the possibilities *currently* offered our Party of penetrating and working inside the fascist organization and among the masses that it influences, but that would oblige me to make a complete analysis of the situation in Italy and of the tasks of the Party—something which would go beyond the scope of this article. One example will suffice. Since the last wage cuts (ordered with a decree in the spring of this year but applied up to now in a way that has been far from uniform so as to allow for the resistance of the working masses and not provoke an unduly large number of simultaneous protests, demonstrations and struggles), the workers' discontent and their will to struggle have been rising rapidly, especially in big industry. The pressure of the working masses on the fascist organization is growing too. It has found expression in violent protests by the workers in union meetings, in the numerous shop committees the workers have named in the factories to present and defend their demands, etc. It also has found expression in a certain number of demonstrations and of episodes of open struggle against the bosses and the Fascists (work stoppages, sit-down strikes, etc.). What are fascism's fears in the face of this situation? Fascism is afraid that this discontent and this thrust of the working masses may develop into a series of open struggles which, while often staring out in great measure on the terrain of and from within the fascist organization itself, may eventually go beyond its compass and *break the fascist legality*. To keep the struggle waged by the masses and directed by the Communist Party from reaching this scope, fascism, as usual, is resorting to a dual action. On the one hand, a stepping up of terror. We already know of two cases in Lombardy in which workers, after participating *en masse* in the fascist meetings and electing a shop committee, called a sit-down strike because none of their demands had been met. The factory's various departmtents were therupon occupied by the guards, who forced the workers to resume work by means of threats and violence. In Milan, where discontent is greatest and is manifested openly, several hundred arrests have been made in the working-class neighborhoods. But at the same time fascism is launching a new maneuver: it is suddenly announcing that from now on, workers affiliated with the fascist unions will have the right (with many reservations, of course) to elect the secretaries of their locals, and that locals will be able to conclude labor contracts. (Before, this right belonged only to the regional or national unions.) This maneuver is linked to an action which is developing on a much vaster political terrain, and which consists in obtaining the open collaboration of a very important group of old leaders of the reformist party by offering them a certain freedom of propaganda and some positions in the fascist apparatus (in the trade-unnion apparatus, first of all) on the sole condition that they accept the principles of the corporative regime. In all likelihood, one of the aims fascism is pursuing is to present some old, very well-known Socialist leaders to the masses as candidates for top-level posts in big locals. How can this political action of fascism, which is developing, as usual, on different levels and through highly varied methods, be countered? It's evident that it cannot be countered effectively except by adeptly and courageously combining the Party's and the class unions' illegal work with the broadest utilization of the legal possibilies.

The Party must rely resolutely on the masses' discontent and their will to struggle. Using every means, it must strive to stimulate the masses' struggle even for the most limited demands, which arise every day in every factory, in every shop. Stepping up their illegal agitation, the Party and the CGL must expose the maneuvers and the demagogy of the Fascists, show on the basis of concrete facts what is hidden behind these maneuvers and this demagogy, and clearly point to the necessity and the objectives of the struggle to overthrow the dictatorship. At the same time, they must expose those Social Democratic leaders who are ready to give open support to the fascist regime. The united-front action we have conducted toward social democracy's emigré leadership has already aided us and will aid us a great deal in all these cases, since it is helping us strongly to bring down the barriers that previously divided Communist workers from Social Democratic workers and to restore the confidence of the workers in general in their forces. Every step we make ahead in forging rank-and-file unity of action among the workers of all political currents in the immediate struggle for the workers' demands and against fascism is an obstacle to the development of the fascist maneuvers, a step in the direction of loosing bigger struggles than the ones being waged today. But all this political and organizational activity of the Party would be insufficient if it were not accompanied by *the most vast and courageous utilization of the legal possibilities* afforded by fascism's maneuvers themselves. To speak concretely: the Communist vanguard must utilize elections of union secretaries, wherever they are held, and even more so the very regulations the Fascists apply to the structures of their unions, to stir, influence and direct vast semi-legal and legal agitation; to strengthen the currents of discontent and of avowed opposition within the unions; to mobilize the masses; to popularize the slogans of the economic and political struggle against fascism; to broaden the front of mass combat; to make the *breaking of the fascist legality*—the scope of all our action and one of the fundamental conditions for giving a frankly and resolutely revolutionary character to the struggle against fascism—approach rapidly. The results of our action will surely be great and favorable provided we work energetically and give proof of activity in all the directions I have just indicated. Fascism's offensive to further reduce the workers' standard of living will then run up against greater and greater resistance; the difficulties it will have to deal with will grow unceasingly; its capacity to maneuver will narrow considerably; its demagogy will be exposed in fact by the action of the masses; and fascism will not fail to get entangled in the web of its own maneuvers. In the face of the difficult situation created for the regime by the struggle of the masses, the hesitations in the ruling spheres of the bourgeoisie will only increase. The conflicts among the various groups of the bourgeoisie will sharpen, which definitely will help enlarge the masses' and the Party's possibilities of struggle and enable us to rise up. The fundamental contradiction between the fascist dictatorship's class character and the masses that fascism endeavors to influence will surface more and more openly and brutally. The dictatorship's whole political and organizational system will be shaken by all this. But none of these results can be reached if we do not eliminate the attitude of opportunistic expectancy and passivity; if we remain turned inward on ourselves like a sect, cut off from the masses, incapable of wide-ranging political action to tie up with them, to direct them.

reference notes

lecture 1: The Basic Features of the Fascist Dictatorship

1. Amadeo Bordiga (1889-1971), whose blanket opposition to parliamentarianism and advocacy of a boycott of all elections Lenin criticized severely in *"Left-Wing" Communism, an Infantile Disorder*, spearheaded the organization of the Communist faction in the Italian Socialist Party and ultimately led it out of the PSI to found the Communist Party of Italy in January 1921. Under Bordiga, the PCI, in a healthy reaction to the worst in the traditions of Italian socialism, stressed the Leninist concept of rigid party discipline and organization. But the Italian Communists' concern with these matters was so great at times that their concrete political action suffered in the end. Furthermore, Bordiga's sectarianism and schematic oversimplification kept the Party from making a deeper analysis of fascism and of the substantive change brought about by the March on Rome. At the Comintern's Fourth World Congress in November 1922, only weeks after the March on Rome, Bordiga asserted that fascism did not represent a qualitatively new development in the history of bourgeois reaction and that the fascist seizure of power would, if anything, simplify the proletariat's task. Bordiga was arrested in Italy in February 1923, whereupon the International, increasingly unhappy with his politics, appointed a new five-man Party Executive. Acquitted and released from prison later that year, Bordiga refused the International's plans of co-opting him into the PCI's new "center" leadership. Meanwhile, Antonio Gramsci, who had remained in the background until then and had more or less accepted Bordiga's policies, gradually formed the nucleus of what would become the PCI's new inner circle of leaders in mid-1924. Bordiga was finally expelled from the Party in 1930. A detailed chronicle of the events surrounding the PCI's birth, the transition from Bordiga to Gramsci, and the positions of Bordiga, Gramsci, Togliatti and others in

the crucial years following the First World War can be found in the introduction to *Selections from the Prison Notebooks of Antonio Gramsci,* edited and translated by Quintin Hoare and Geoffrey Nowell Smith (International Publishers, New York 1971).

2. Filippo Turati (1857-1932) led the Italian Socialist Party from its foundation in 1892. His theoretical and political positions were typical of the reformist degeneration of the Second International. Under him, the PSI entered into a tacit alliance with the Northern industrial bourgeoisie. After the First World War, Turati fought the vain revolutionary rhetoric of his party's then-ascendant maximalist wing. But whereas the Communists' quarrel with the maximalists centered on the latter's ineffectualness as revolutionaries, Turati was interested in an alternative to socialist revolution and thus saw the maximalists as the major roadblock to a progressive reform coalition with the more enlightened strata of the bourgeoisie and petty bourgeoisie. Expelled from the PSI in October 1922, Turati helped found the reformist Italian Unitary Socialist Party (PSUI). He fled to France in 1926 when the wave of "extraordinary laws" erased the last traces of pre-fascist democracy in Italy.

Claudio Treves (1858-1933) was Turati's closest collaborator in the PSI. Also expelled in October 1922, Treves followed Turati into the new reformist party and, like him, was forced into exile in 1926.

3. See Ercoli, "Contro le false analogie tra situazione tedesca e situazione italiana," *Lo Stato Operaio*, VI, 9 (September 1932), pp. 516-529, now in Palmiro Togliatti, *Sul movimento operaio internazionale*, ed. Franco Ferri (*Editori Riuniti*, Rome 1964), pp. 63-82.

4. The Right-wing riots in France on February 6, 1934, quelled by the police, helped awaken the French Left and the International to the threat of a further spread of fascist regimes. The event was therefore instrumental in paving the way to the Popular Front policy.

5. *Giustizia e Libertà*, an anti-fascist movement founded in late 1929 by Carlo Rosselli, Emilio Lussu, Riccardo Bauer and other middle-class intellectuals, combined secularism, voluntarism, republicanism and radicalism in an eclectic, activist ideology. Its program called for a republican form of government, regional autonomy, bureaucratic reform and a mixed economy. In 1942, the core group of the movement formed the Action Party, which disbanded in 1947 after having played an important role in the armed resistance to fascism and nazism.

6. See note 3 on p. 160.

7. The Popular Party, forerunner of today's Christian Democratic Party, was founded in January 1919 with active support from the Vatican. It became Italy's second-largest party in the 1919 and 1921 elec-

tions, developing a mass base mainly among the peasantry. Popularism arose as a Catholic reaction to liberalism on the one hand and socialism on the other. Conservative in its goal of stemming the Socialists' post-war advance, the Popular Party was in effect "subversive" in its opposition to the traditional liberal state. Although its leader, Luigi Sturzo, was an anti-fascist, Vatican pressure forced the party into an ambiguous stand on the regime. The Popular Party was suppressed along with the other opposition parties in 1925-26 after the Matteotti crisis.

8. *Fasci italiani di combattimento* (Italian Fighting Leagues) was the official name Mussolini's movement took after its constituent meeting in Milan on March 23, 1919.

9. The history of alternating political cooperation and rivalry between Mussolini and Socialist leader Pietro Nenni (b. 1891) dated back to 1908 when Nenni, then a Republican, was head of the Forli farm laborers' union while Mussolini was secretary of the Socialist Party's Forli chapter. Both men pushed for Italian intervention in World War I on the side of the Entente, a position for which Mussolini was expelled from the PSI. After the war, Nenni participated in the constituent meeting of Bologna's democratic *fascio di combattimento*. The Bologna organization propounded a radical, democratic solution to the problems of the ex-servicemen and the petty bourgeoisie—a sign of the original ambivalence of the mass movement that Mussolini was attempting to harness. Nenni subsequently gravitated to a more definite class position, joining the PSI in 1921.

10. The fascist movement was officially born in a meeting held on March 23, 1919 in a hall on Milan's Piazza San Sepolcro. The event brought together under a single program the group gathered around Mussolini's newspaper *Il Popolo d'Italia*, futurists, demobilized servicemen and an anarcho-syndicalist minority. The resulting program was a demagogic hodgepodge of nationalism and vague social reform: the movement defined itself as anti-imperialist, but openly defended the World War and upheld the Italian claims to Fiume (Rijeka) and Dalmatia; it stated its objective was to further the cause of labor, but proclaimed itself anti-socialist and anti-democratic. Symptomatic is the fact that the concept of "productivism," i.e. capital's supremacy and labor's subjugation to the necessities of private property and profit, was adopted by the movement and included in the program. The program's ambiguity made it unable to compete with the Socialist Party's mass line on the one hand, or to convince the capitalists to give the new movement immediate backing on the other. This inherent weakness led to the fiasco in the November 16, 1919 general elections, when the only all-Fascist slate, running in Milan, received a grand total of 4,795 votes.

11. The word *squadrismo* was coined to describe the organized, systematic violence employed by the fascist "action squads."

12. The mass occupation of the machine and metal factories of Turin, Milan, Genoa and scores of lesser industrial centers at the beginning of September 1920, ordered by the Italian Metalworkers' Federation (FIOM) in response to an industry-wide lockout, is generally depicted as the high-water mark of Italy's postwar revolutionary tide. Certainly, the question whether or not the takeover movement (which spread to other industries and was actively backed by the railwaymen) represented the ripe opportunity for revolution is still debated. The occupation of the factories ended in a temporary trade-union victory for the metalworkers, but its broader political consequences for the workers' movement as a whole were disastrous: the Socialist Party's unpreparedness and basic unwillingness to "make the revolution" were exposed; the energies of the Italian working class were sorely taxed; and the industrialists turned *en masse* to fascism in order to protect their class privileges. An anarchist, Luigi Fabbri, called this last-mentioned phenomenon—the capitalist reaction once the revolutionary floodwave had crested and was receding—the basis of the "preventive counter-revolution."

13. The *fasci italiani di combattimento* transformed themselves into the National Fascist Party at the conclusion of the congress held in Rome's Teatro Augusteo from November 7 to 10, 1921. The step was more or less forced on Mussolini by the movement's intransigent wing.

14. After the First World War, Italian industry and commerce and the Italian military establishment set their eyes on the city of Fiume (Rijeka) on the Dalmatian coast as the key to turning the Adriatic into an "Italian lake" and opening up the territories of the former Austro-Hungarian Empire to economic penetration. Irredentist forces led by poet Gabriele D'Annunzio (1863-1938) occupied the city in September 1919 while the territorial dispute with Yugoslavia was still pending. Under D'Annunzio's control, Fiume became a hotbed of sedition against the government in Rome. Mussolini backed the poet's move and was informed of his schemes regarding a "march on Rome" to begin with a troop landing on Italy's east coast. The Fiume question was resolved, however, in November 1920 by the Treaty of Rapallo, which as part of the settlement of Italian-Yugoslav border issues made Fiume an independent city-state. Faced with this *fait accompli*, Mussolini tempered his support for D'Annunzio and finally betrayed the poet by revealing the coup d'état plans in his newspaper. The fact that D'Annunzio's direct action had lifted the poet to the No. 1 position in the pantheon of the right-wing subversive movement no doubt goes a

long way to explaining Mussolini's about-face. The occupation of Fiume ended on December 26, 1920 when an Italian military force, on orders from Premier Giovanni Giolitti, chased D'Annunzio's "legionnaires" out of the city.

lecture 2: The Bourgeoisie's "New Type of Party"

1. Giacomo Matteotti (1885-1924), secretary of the reformist Unitary Socialist Party, was abducted and killed by a band of Fascists on June 10, 1924 because of a speech he had delivered on May 30 in the Chamber of Deputies denouncing violence and fraud in the general elections held earlier that year. News of Matteotti's disappearance—his body was not found until mid-August—sent shockwaves of indignation and rebellion throughout the country. The opposition parties walked out of Parliament, meeting on the Aventine in a Committee of the Oppositions. The PCI, militant and anxious to seize the initiative, but numerically weak and saddled with the Bordiga leadership's legacy of sectarianism, called for mass action and a general strike to topple Mussolini's tottering regime. The Communists' appeal, however, was officially rebuffed on June 18 by the reformist-led General Confederation of Labor and by all the other political parties represented on the Committee, from the Socialists to the Liberal Democrats. As a result, the PCI withdrew from the Committee. Mussolini stalled for time. He had the Fascists who were most directly implicated in Matteotti's slaying to formally reduce the PNF's direct role in the government. Meanwhile, the Aventine parties' basic weaknesses became apparent: their fear of mobilizing the masses, their abstract moralizing, their hope in the legal indictment or at least the ouster of Mussolini, and their general reluctance to take any positive action enabled Mussolini, buoyed by a fresh onslaught of *squadrismo*, to consolidate his position as the crisis wore on. The tacit support offered the regime by the Vatican, the leading capitalist interests and King Victor Emanuel III finally tipped the balance in the Duce's favor. When the Chamber of Deputies reopened on January 3, 1925, Mussolini took the offensive, assuming full responsibility for all of fascism's actions. His speech marked the end of the transitional period during which the Fascists had paid lip-service to the structures of the liberal state, and the start of intensive measures to reorganize the regime on a totalitarian basis.

2. Francesco Saverio Nitti (1868-1953), an economist and Radical politician from Lucania, was Premier of Italy from June 1919 to June 1920.

3. Giovanni Giolitti (1842-1928), Premier in 1892-93, 1906-09, 1911-14 and 1920-21, was the dominant figure in Italian politics after the turn of the century. In the unfinished essay *Alcuni temi della quistione meridionale*, Gramsci makes a strikingly clear and concise analysis of Giolitti's ascent and the mechanism of his domestic policy: "After the bloody decade of 1890-1900, the bourgeoisie had to forgo an overly exclusivistic, overly violent, overly direct dictatorship; the Southern peasants and Northern workers were rising up in revolt against it *simultaneously* although not in coordination. With the new century, the ruling class inaugurated a new policy—of class alliances, of class political blocs, i.e. of bourgeois democracy. It had to choose: either a rural democracy, that is to say an alliance with the Southern peasants, a policy of free trade, universal suffrage, administrative decentralization and low prices on industrial products; or a capitalist-worker bloc without universal suffrage, for tariff protectionism, for the preservation of state centralization (the expression of bourgeois rule over the peasants, especially those of the South and of the islands), for a reformist policy of wages and labor rights. It chose—not by chance—the second solution. Giolitti personified bourgeois rule; the Socialist Party became the instrument of Giolitti's policy." Antonio Gramsci, *Scritti politici* (Editori Riuniti, Rome 1967), p. 729.

A campaign speech Giolitti delivered in Dronero on October 19, 1919 represented the most progressive bourgeois proposal for solving Italy's postwar crisis. In this speech, Giolitti criticized Italy's intervention in the war, harking back to his neutralist positions of 1914-15 (whence Togliatti's reference to the nationalists' accusation that Giolitti had been a "defeatist traitor"); called for reform of Art. 5 of the Statute of Carl Albert in order to deprive the king and the cabinet of the power to declare war, and confer that power on Parliament; pledged progressive income and inheritance taxes and the compulsory registration of corporate shares; threatened private industry with possible state intervention to expand hydroelectric production; and propounded putting an end to state control of foreign trade. Essentially, the Dronero speech embodied Giolitti's program for saving the bourgeoisie's economic and political power within the liberal-democratic framework by broadening the state's base and thereby blunting the advance of the revolutionary movement. By 1920, however, with Giolitti again Premier, the situation had already changed, and the elderly statesman was unable to see that the growing fascist movement posed a threat not only to the revolutionary movement, but also to the liberal state that he wished to preserve. Giolitti tried to exploit *squadrismo* as a counterweight to the workers' movement, and opened the doors of Parliament to the Fascists by including them in the electoral alliances he formed for the 1921 elections.

4. A nationally influential newspaper of liberal persuasion.

5. The Fascists and Socialists signed a truce—the "pacification pact"—on August 3, 1921. Despite major resistance from his followers, Mussolini advocated signing the pact for a complex series of tactical reasons. The pact caused a drastic split between the urban *fasci* led by Mussolini, closer to industrial interests, and the outlying organizations, more concerned with direct action to suppress the vast farm workers' and rural cooperative movement. Mussolini was forced to resign from the Executive Committee of the *fasci di combattimento* on August 15; two days later, the Fascist hard-liners met in Bologna to coordinate their action. After a while, feeling that the pact had served its purpose, Mussolini characteristically changed sides. He was officially won over to the intransigents' position at the Fascists' Rome Congress in November, declaring the pact null and void on November 15.

6. The members of the Communist faction walked out of the PSI's 27th Congress, held in Livorno from January 15 to 21, 1921, to found the PCI.

7. The volunteer commandos in the Italian army were called *arditi*. In July 1921, former *arditi* joined in a group to combat fascist violence. Taking the name *Arditi del popolo*, the group soon attracted many militant Communists, Socialists and anarchists, and grew from its original nucleus into a mass armed self-defense organization of the working class. This development, however, took place completely outside of party lines. Official opposition to the new organization came not only from the PSI, which was busy negotiating the pacification pact with the Fascists, but also from the PCI. The PCI took the sectarian position that Communist workers should join only its own Red Guard. This combined Socialist and Communist hostility undermined what in effect was a genuine grass-roots rebellion against fascism and put the rank-and-file Socialists and Communists who had eagerly joined the *Arditi del popolo* in an untenable position, forcing most of them to withdraw. Lacking strong political leadership, the organization quickly declined, surviving only on a local level in certain cities.

8. Premier Luigi Facta's government fell on July 19, 1922. On July 28, at the height of the government crisis, and as fascist forces were laying waste to Ravenna, the Socialist Party's parliamentary group, composed mainly of reformists soon to be expelled from the party, passed a resolution to the effect that the PSI would give parliamentary support to a government which would restore order and guarantee basic democratic rights. Filippo Turati went to the Quirinal Palace the next day to convey this untimely offer of class collaboration to King

Victor Emanuel III, but the situation remained unresolved. Facta eventually formed a second cabinet, whose life was terminated only three months later by the March on Rome.

9. With a speech delivered in Udine on September 20, 1922, Mussolini eliminated the last official traces of what had been the fascist movement's and party's tendentially pro-republican, anti-monarchist stance.

10. See note 4 on p. 156.

11. Bruno Buozzi (1881-1944), a reformist deputy and trade-unionist, led the Italian Metalworkers' Federation at the time of the September 1920 occupation of the factories. After years of exile, Buozzi returned to Italy in July 1943 as head of the reorganized General Confederation of Labor. He was slain by the Nazis on June 6, 1944 on the outskirts of Rome just as the German rear guard was withdrawing from the capital.

Gino Baldesi (1879-1934), a reformist deputy, was one of the most powerful figures in the CGL's leadership. In the period immediately preceding the fascist seizure of power, Baldesi urged abrogation of the unity-of-action pact between the CGL and the Socialist Party. This was obtained when the reformists, including most of the CGL's top officials, were thrown out of the PSI in October 1922. During the first years of fascist rule, Mussolini toyed with the idea of including Baldesi in his cabinet. Furthermore, Baldesi's name cropped up in connection with schemes to merge the class unions with the fascist labor organizations. A more marked anti-fascist tone characterized Baldesi's positions after 1924.

12. Roberto Farinacci (1892-1945), Fascist chieftain of Cremona, a leader of the movement's intransigent rural wing. In 1924, towards the end of the Matteotti crisis, Farinacci organized the resurgence of violence that covered Mussolini's flank while the Duce maneuvered to retain power. A grateful Mussolini named him secretary of the PNF on February 12, 1925, but forced him to resign two years later when Farinacci's positions ran afoul of the big bourgeoisie. Farinacci retreated to his Cremona stronghold and thereafter was a marginal figure in the regime until the period just before Italy's entry in World War II. He was executed by Italian partisans in 1945.

13. Luigi Federzoni (1875-1967), one of the founders of the pre-fascist Italian Nationalist Association, joined the PNF in the 1923 Fascist-Nationalist fusion. After serving as Minister of the Colonies in Mussolini's first cabinet, he was named Minister of the Interior in June 1924. It was in this capacity that he clashed with Farinacci over the latter's idea of strict party primacy over the state.

Alfredo Rocco (1875-1935), another Nationalist the PNF absorbed in 1923. As Minister of Justice from 1925 to 1932, he supervised the drafting of the legislation that established totalitarianism in every branch of the state and of society. The laws on the press, public security and political associations, the Charter of Labor and other corporativist documents, and the new penal code all bore the imprint of Rocco's conception of reactionary state control.

lecture 3: The National Fascist Party

1. Leonida Bissolati and other extreme right-wing reformists who had supported Giolitti's increasingly aggressive colonialist policy in 1911-12, particularly the conquest of Libya, were expelled from the Socialist Party at its 12th National Congress in Reggio, Emilia in July 1912. Control of the party passed into the hands of the maximalist wing led by Costantino Lazzari and Giacinto Menotti Serrati.

2. See note 7 on p. 156.

3. Giuseppe Bottai (1895-1959) was one of the intellectuals most actively committed to forging an organic ideology for the regime. As Undersecretary of Corporations from 1926 to 1929 and Minister of Corporations from 1929 to 1932, Bottai engaged in the pursuit of a chimerical economic system qualitatively different from both socialism and capitalism. Bottai, who initially was an admirer of the New Deal, was obviously unable to resolve the contradiction between his schemes of limited economic democracy under the tutelage of the state, and the brutal reality of bourgeois political and economic dictatorship under fascism. Mussolini ousted him from the government in 1932 after Bottai opposed the creation of additional "emergency" mechanisms designed to prop up industries in a way restrictive of production. Later, Bottai served as Minister of Education from 1936 to 1943, and voted against Mussolini on July 25, 1943 in the session of the Grand Council of Fascism in which the regime practically dissolved itself.

4. Walter Beneduce (1877-1944), a member of Bissolati's Social Reformist Party and Minister of Labor in 1921-22, started drifting toward open collaboration with the fascist regime in 1925. Beneduce, who earlier had set up a group of quasi-public credit institutions to finance utilities and public works, was the man behind the formation of the Institute for Industrial Reconstruction in 1933. IRI was devised as a bail-out operation for faltering banks and industries, but later became a real public industrial holding company. Public ownership did not, however, do away with the joint-stock form of property, and IRI's subsidiaries basically continued to be managed as if they were privately-owned companies.

5. Alessandri's group was christened the "Gironde" for its desire to reach an accommodation with the regime. Alessandri (1869-?) soon faded into obscurity.

6. Antonio Salandra (1853-1931), an ultra-conservative politician and spokesman for the Apulian landowning class, was Premier from 1914 to 1916. He and his political mentor, Foreign Minister Sidney Sonnino, secretly arranged for Italy's entry in World War I. There was strong popular opposition to intervention, but Salandra and Sonnino saw it as an opportunity to bolster the state's repressive powers under wartime conditions. In September 1922, Salandra proclaimed himself an "honorary Fascist."

7. See note 1 on p. 170.

8. Pasquini was the *nom de guerre* of Secondino Tranquilli, known today as Ignazio Silone. Silone was removed from the PCI's Central Committee in 1930 and expelled from the Party in July 1931. Togliatti's reference to Silone as an authority therefore must have had a certain shock value. The article in question appeared in the PCI's theoretical monthly, Secondino Tranquilli, "Elementi per uno studio del P.N.F. (Borghesia, piccola borghesia e fascismo)," *Lo Stato Operaio*, I, 8 (Oct. 1927), pp. 875-890. Interestingly enough, fascism's assimilation of other political forces as outlined in this lesson by Togliatti (and probably as set forth in the students' "material") follows the seven-point scheme contained in another article by Silone: Secondino Tranquilli, "Borghesia, piccola borghesia e fascismo," *Lo Stato Operaio*, II, 4 (April 1928), pp. 150-160.

9. The contradictions in the Fascist Party's heterogeneous base started to generate centrifugal tendencies almost immediately after the March on Rome. The Fascists had seized power without a well-defined program. Mussolini tried to compensate for this by performing his eternal juggling act between old-line Nationalists and monarchists on the one hand, and the petty-bourgeois cadres who wanted to remake the state under party dictatorship on the other. The crisis between the "normalizers" and the "intransigents" came to a head in May 1923. Although couched in ideological and programmatic terms, the dispute revealed the underlying personal ambition and rancor of the various faction leaders. Perhaps feeling that he had allowed the return to normalcy to go too far, Mussolini temporarily sided with the intransigents.

Cesare Forni and Raimondo Sala, top *squadristi* on the payroll of the big agrarian interests of northwestern Italy, were opposed to a compromise with the pre-fascist politicians. Alfredo Misuri, who had been forced out of the PNF in Perugia but later rejoined it in the Fascist-Nationalist fusion, spoke instead for conservative agrarian interests tied to a more orthodox authoritarianism. On May 29, 1923 Misuri delivered a speech denouncing the PNF's usurpation of state power and interference with normal administrative functions. Six hours later he was beaten up by a gang of thugs dispatched by Mussolini.

10. See note 1 on p. 159.

11. See note 8 on p. 166.

lecture 4: Fascism's Military and Propaganda Organizations

1. Instituted in April 1926, Opera Nazionale Balilla was the umbrella agency through which the regime controlled the out-of-school activities of Italian children and youth. Originally, it was structured into a series of parallel organizations for boys (*Balilla,* who at age fourteen became Vanguardists and received premilitary training) and girls (Little Italians, who graduated to become Young Italians). In 1930, a Young Fascists division was set up for youths age eighteen to twenty-one.

2. The Fascists conceived the Opera Nazionale Balilla as a state monopoly of all youth organizations. To achieve this goal, the regime had to dismantle the Catholic youth groups. The first inroads were made against the Catholic Boy Scouts, which were disbanded in a series of decrees between 1926 and 1928. In 1931, the regime launched a major attack against all of the Catholic Action organizations whose activities touched on social, labor or political issues, two of its principal targets being the Society of Italian Catholic Youth and the Italian Catholic University Federation. Pope Pius XI published an encyclical protesting the violence of this campaign but not fundamentally condemning fascism. Shortly thereafter, negotiations were begun which led to an accord under which the Vatican severely curtailed the Catholic organizations' concern with non-spiritual matters and took measures to steer them away from anti-fascism. As far as the youth associations in particular were concerned, the Vatican agreed to limit their sphere of action exclusively to "recreational and educational activities having religious purposes."

3. University cultural and art competitions which were held yearly from 1934 to 1940 on a national scale. The oral debates on a wide variety of subjects ranging from poetry to foreign policy proved to be a breeding ground for many young anti-fascists.

4. For Cesare Forni, see note 9 on p. 164. Aurelio Padovani, undisputed head of the Fascist Party and Fascist Militia in Naples and Campania, fell from grace in May 1923 in the clash between the "normalizers" and the "intransigents." Padovani believed that the merger with the Nationalists meant a betrayal of fascism's "revolutionary" origins and would buttress the pre-fascist power structure in the South. His anti-monarchical and anti-bourgeois pronouncements made him a definite liability for the new regime. During the Matteotti crisis, Farinacci asked Padovani to rejoin the PNF, but he declined.

5. The pet idea of Mario Giampaoli, one of the founders of the *fasci italiani di combattimento* in 1919 and head of the PNF's Milan province organization in the 1920s, had been to form party cells at the factory level in order to bring production workers into the party.

6. Hitler liquidated his opponents in the Nazi Party on June 30, 1934. Ernst Röhm and other leaders of the SA were the principal victims of the bloodbath.

7. See note 1 on p. 159.

8. Leandro Arpinati (1892-1945), originally an intransigent and Undersecretary of the Interior from September 1929 to May 1933, was expelled from the PNF together with a small band of followers on May 4, 1933. Arpinati was sentenced the next year to five years of forced domicile on charges of conspiring against Mussolini. He was killed by partisans on April 22, 1945 near Bologna. Arpinati's organized dissidence centered on his opposition to the expansion of the state's role in the economy and, at the same time, to the PNF's encroachment on the functions of the state.

lecture 5: **Fascist Trade Unions**

1. *Dopolavoro,* literally "after-work," the system of recreational and free-time organizations that the regime set up for the workers. See the lesson on the Dopolavoro below.

2. The anarcho-syndicalists cut their ties with the Socialist Party and the General Confederation of Labor in 1907, founding the Italian Syndical Union (USI). In 1914, in the dispute over the labor movement's position on Italian entry in the First World War, pro-intervention syndicalists broke away from the USI.

3. Enrico Ferri (1856-1929), originally a Socialist, then a syndicalist, gravitated to fascism in 1922 and ended up as an apologist for Mussolini. Arturo Labriola, the most significant Italian anarcho-syndicalist, was a supporter in 1911 of the colonial conquest of Libya and in 1914 of

Italian intervention in World War I. He served as Giolitti's Minister of Labor in 1920-21. An anti-fascist, Labriola was elected to the Senate in 1948 after the Liberation.

4. Edmondo Rossoni, an anarcho-syndicalist who had been active in the Industrial Workers of the World while living in the United States. Rossoni returned to Italy in 1915 and joined the fascist movement in 1921. He was head of the Confederation of Fascist Trade Unions from 1922 to 1928, and Minister of Agriculture from 1935 to 1939.

5. Luigi Razza (1892-1935) was president of the Fascist Confederation of Agricultural Unions. Mussolini named him Minister of Public Works in 1935 as part of a cabinet shuffle in preparation for the attack on Ethiopia, but Razza died soon afterward in an airplane crash.

6. The General Confederation of Labor.

7. The Italian Metalworkers' Federation, affiliated with the CGdL.

8. The reformist heads of the General Confederation of Labor voluntarily dissolved the organization on January 4, 1927. The Communists then called a clandestine meeting in Milan on February 20 to rebuild the class labor center's national policy-making structure.

9. The Vidoni Palace Pact between the Confederation of Industry and the fascist trade unions, signed on October 2, 1925, gave the latter the exclusive right to represent workers in collective bargaining with industries belonging to the Confederation, and set the stage for the dismantling of shop committee and the disbanding of non-fascist trade unions.

The Law of April 3, 1926 granted juridical status to the Confederation of Industry and the management associations in the other sectors of the economy, and completely suppressed the workers' contractual freedom by establishing that official recognition of the fascist unions and management associations meant that contracts signed between them were binding even on non-members. At the same time, the right to strike was abrogated.

The Charter of Labor, approved by the Grand Council of Fascism on April 21, 1927, was really not a law but an ideological declaration aimed at filling the void left by the ban on democratic labor organizations. A vague corporativist manifesto, the Charter pretended to resolve the contradictions between labor and capital by subsuming both in the higher concept of "the Nation." It defined work as a "social duty" while offering no concrete guarantees to the workers in the form of minimum wages, etc. Legislative implementation of the Charter's principles was put in the hands of the government, which used this power to erect the authoritarian, bureaucratic structure of the corporative state.

10. The Law of April 3, 1926 meant the death of what once had been a wide network of Catholic labor unions. On April 19, 1926, Catholic Action authorized its members to join the fascist unions and fell back on the idea of creating trade groups to conduct study, welfare and training activities. With the outbreak of the economic crisis, these groups tended to enlarge their field of interest and were consequently attacked by spokesmen for the fascist unions and the corporative structure. Finally, under a September 1931 pact with the state, the Vatican agreed that Catholic Action would not try to set up professional associations or trade unions. The Vatican also pledged to limit the study groups to spiritual and religious matters, and to see that they would assist the corporative organizations in ensuring class collaboration.

11. In the first plebiscite, held on March 24, 1929, the country was asked to approve the Lateran Pacts with the Vatican. Five years later, on March 25, 1934, the regime held a second plebiscite as a substitute for parliamentary elections. Voters were asked to respond with a simple yes or no to the question: "Do you approve the list of deputies designated by the Grand Council of Fascism?"

lecture 6: The "Dopolavoro"

1. The name Dopolavoro applied both to the system of free-time organizations that the regime operated for the workers and to the individual clubs, circles or centers belonging to that system. The National Dopolavoro Agency, founded in 1925, had six main operating divisions concerned with organization, administration, sports, excursions, the arts and welfare.

2. A group of traveling theatrical companies that the regime set up in 1928 to give open-air performances throughout Italy.

3. The Communist Youth International.

lecture 7: Corporativism

1. The fascist regime's nomenclature and the myths it created about its economic structures engendered considerable confusion, in part deliberate, in part reflecting the muddy nature of the fascist ideology. The reader will find this lesson on corporativism more readily comprehensible if he bears in mind that the term *corporazione* (corporation or guild) was applied to a wide variety of institutions from 1922 to 1943. Similarly, the world *sindacato* (syndicate or union) was used to define both employers' and employees' associations. (The lat-

ter, in reality, were trade unions, and are translated accordingly in the present volume.) The word *corporazione* was first employed in January 1922, when the Fascists, not yet in power, decided that all fascist "syndicates" would be grouped under five "Corporations" covering all professional, manual and technical activities. The employers' and employees' associations, however, were not merged. These corporations, also called "mixed syndicates," remained a reality in name only. The employers' and employees' associations continued to operate independently of each other.

The regime established a Minister of Corporations on July 2, 1926, but did not create corporations until 1931, when the National Council of Corporations, set up the year before, was divided into seven sections, called "corporations," dealing with the specific problems of agriculture, industry, commerce, maritime transport, land transport, credit and insurance, and the professions. Finally, on February 5, 1934, the regime instituted twenty-two "sectorial corporations." These lumped together the "producers" of raw materials, finished goods and services, and the wholesale and retail merchants, engaged in each of twenty-two specific "cycles" (cereals, wood, textiles, construction, utilities, insurance and credit, domestic communications, etc.). The governing bodies of the sectorial corporations included 268 councillors representing the capitalists, 268 hand-picked by the regime to represent the workers, 66 speaking directly for the Fascist Party, and an indefinite number of experts and senior bureaucrats.

2. See note 1 on p. 170.

3. Ugo Spirito, an idealist philosopher and theorist of corporativism, launched the idea of the "corporation as property" at the Second Conference of Syndical and Corporative Studies, held in Ferrara from March 5 to 8, 1932. Spirito foresaw the resolution of the contradiction between the individual and the state, and between capital and labor, in a "post-capitalist" corporative economy. According to his scheme, the state's role would not be so much to mediate between capital and labor as to merge them, the basic structure for this being the productive corporation, shares in which would be distributed to the workers "in accordance with their particular hierarchic ranks." Capitalist interests not directly operative in the organization and management of production would thus tend to be expropriated. The label "left-wing corporativism" applied to Spirito's ideas was in reality inappropriate inasmuch as Spirito's plan would have done away even with the fascist trade unions, thereby stripping the workers of the structure within which they could assert what little bargaining power they had left. Furthermore, it would have made the workers' pay (in the form of

"profits" under the profit-sharing system) depend strictly on the fortunes of their companies.

4. Here, *corporazione* is translated as *guild*.

5. The Socialist Party's official daily, published in Paris after it had been suppressed in Italy in October 1926.

6. The encyclical *Rerum novarum*, published by Pope Leo XIII on May 15, 1891, represented the Catholic Church's first major official attempt to theorize its intervention in the sphere of social problems caused by the nineteenth-century expansion of capitalism and the accompanying growth of the workers' movement. An anti-socialist document at heart, the encyclical defined property as a God-given natural right and solicited the state to act in its defense. The encyclical was considerably less specific regarding the public authorities' role in protecting labor, although it did vaguely call for some regulation of holidays, working hours, child labor, etc. While not taking sides in the debate then current in Catholic circles over the choice between Catholic trade unions and mixed guilds of employers and employees, and in fact expressing a theoretical preference for the latter, it realistically granted Catholic union organizers a certain freedom of action.

Quadragesimo anno, the encyclical issued by Pope Pius XI on May 15, 1931 to celebrate the fortieth anniversary of the publication of *Rerum novarum* and fill out its content in light of the intervening developments, praised the fascist corporative system for guaranteeing orderly class collaboration and suppressing the socialist labor organizations.

7. In this speech, delivered on October 6, 1934, Mussolini called corporativism the only alternative to communism.

8. The PNF's theoretical review, published monthly.

9. Mario Nicoletti, *nom de guerre*, of Giuseppe Di Vittorio, head of the Confederation of Labor after the Second World War. The article in question is: Giuseppe Di Vittorio, "Le corporazioni di categoria," *Lo Stato Operaio*, VII, 9-10 (Sept.-Oct. 1933), pp. 544-556.

10. See note 3 on p. 163.

11. The newspaper published by the fascist trade-union apparatus.

lecture 7 (cont.): Our Policy Toward the Corporations

1. The National Association for the Study of Labor Problems and its review, *Problemi del lavoro*, were founded in 1927 by Rinaldo Rigola, ex-secretary general of the General Confederation of Labor. On January

4 of that year, Rigola and other reformist union leaders had voted to disband the CGdL voluntarily. Twelve days later, Rigola and a band of fellow reformists met in Milan and subscribed to a document promising to contribute with constructive criticism and action to the success of the corporative "experiment." The group said it disavowed neither the reality of the class struggle nor the validity of socialism as an ultimate goal, but gave a positive assessment of the regime's "reforms" (the Law of April 3, 1926 and the then-being-drafted Charter of Labor) and social program. Invoking a false sense of realism in attempting to justify its substantially collaborationist stance, the group asserted in its manifesto that *a priori* opposition to corporativism would not be in the workers' interest, which would best be served by a "pragmatic" approach to fascist social and economic policy. Through the next decade, the review's publication was tolerated by the regime, for the advantages of the ultra-reformists' collaboration more than outweighed the disadvantages of their innocuous criticism. Emilio Caldara, Socialist Mayor of Milan from 1914 to 1920, was a contributor to *Problemi del lavoro.*

2. Antonio Labriola (1843-1904), the Marxist philosopher who influenced the intellectual formation of Benedetto Croce, Gramsci and Togliatti himself. The interview which Togliatti refers to below appeared not in 1904 but on April 13, 1902 in the Rome newspaper *Il Giornale d'Italia.*

3. "Agli operai, ai contadini, ai lavoratori, a tutti gli sfruttati, a tutti gli oppressi dal capitalismo e dal fascismo," *Lo Stato Operaio*, VII, 11-12 (Nov.-Dec. 1933), pp. 621-636.

4. A system of time and motion evaluation devised by the French engineer Charles Bedaux (1888-1944) and used for the first time in 1918 in the United States. Its goal was the maximum intensive exploitation of labor. The Bedaux system, in fact, did not concern itself with capital investment to raise productivity, but aimed only at increasing the speed at which a worker performed a given job. Introduced in Italy in the 1920s, it gained favor with a number of industries as a means of slashing wages by setting higher, "scientifically-determined" production quotas and eliminating overtime.

lecture 8: Fascism's Policy in the Countryside

1. A hectare, or 10,000 square meters, is roughly equivalent to 2.5 acres. A metric quintal, or 100 kilograms, is roughly equivalent to 220.5 pounds.

2. Andrea Marabini, "I risultati della battaglia del grano," *Lo Stato Operaio,* VII, 5 (May 1934), pp. 392-406, and "Spostamenti de classe nelle campagne italiane," *Lo Stato Operaio,* VII, 7 (July 1934), pp. 507-518.

Appendix: Where is the Force of Italian Fascism?

1. *L'Internationale communiste,* XVI, 19 (5 October 1934), pp. 1254-1270. Signed: Ercoli.

2. Lenin, *Selected Works,* 12 vols. (Moscow: Co-operative Publishing Society of Foreign Workers in the U.S.S.R., 1938), vol. 10, p. 333.